This book is dedicated to
' Margot ' Sanger
for whom the only accurate epithet is
Unique

THE PROSODY OF CHAUCER AND HIS FOLLOWERS

THE PROSODY OF CHAUCER AND HIS FOLLOWERS

Supplementary Chapters to
Verses of Cadence

By

JAMES G. SOUTHWORTH

Professor of English, University of Toledo

GREENWOOD PRESS, PUBLISHERS
WESTPORT, CONNECTICUT

Library of Congress Cataloging in Publication Data

Southworth, James Granville, 1896-
    The prosody of Chaucer and his followers.

    Reprint of the ed. published by Blackwell, Oxford.
    1.   Chaucer, Geoffrey, d. 1400--Versification.
2.   English language--Middle English, 1100-1500--Rhythm.
I.   Title.
PR1951.S6 1978   821'.1   77-16835
ISBN 0-313-20008-4

Reprinted with the permission of Basil Blackwell Publisher

Reprinted in 1978 by Greenwood Press, Inc.,
51 Riverside Avenue, Westport, CT. 06880

Printed in the United States of America

CONTENTS

Preface IX

I Ecclesiastical and Secular Influences: Rhythm, Intonation
Punctuation 1

II Chaucer and his Contemporaries 25

III The Canterbury Tales 53

IV Chaucer's Disciples 73

Appendix 79

PREFACE

SINCE writing *Verses of Cadence* I have learned much about the prosody of the Middle Ages which has thrown additional light upon the prosody of Chaucer, Hoccleve, Lydgate, and others. The chief benefit of my investigations has been the ability to give further evidence for the nature of Chaucer's prosody, a theory at which I had arrived as the result of a growing aesthetic dissatisfaction with the conventional way of reading him. I realize, too, that it was a partial theory and did not cover from the point of rhythm all the types of verse that Chaucer used. The prosody of the *ABC* exemplifies the real meaning of verses of cadence, that of *Hous of Fame* a modified one; and that for *Troilus and Criseyde* and the *Canterbury Tales* is essentially a rediscovery of a prosody (over-simplified though it had become) generally accepted until Child's 'Observations' began to exert its influence in the latter part of the 19th C.

Scholars have long been teased by Chaucer's statement:

> To make songes / dytees bookys
> In ryme or elles / in cadence
> As thou best canst / in reverence
> Of love / and of his servants eke
> That have his servyse soght and seke . . .   (622–626)

As the result of curiosity about this statement their scholarly investigations have thrown much light on the origins, meaning, and significance of *cadence* in medieval prose, and particularly that of Chaucer, but none on the meaning as applied to his poetry. I now realize that although Chaucer occasionally uses cadence in the *Troilus* and the *Canterbury Tales*, it is not in general the meaning of *cadence* as understood by the men of the Middle Ages. His prosody in these poems is an outgrowth of the original meaning of the term. And, strictly speaking, I was wrong to apply the term to those poems. The reason that scholars have failed to see the meaning of the term arises from their persistence in clinging to the iambic theory of his versification. The passage about cadence is itself an example of cadence. Line 615 is *cursus trochaicus*, 616 is *cursus planus*, 617, 618, 619 are *cursus tardus*.

There is nothing in the first three chapters of *Verses of Cadence* that I feel needs alteration. Their purpose was to show that the hypotheses on which the metrical theory of Chaucer's prosody were based were not supported by fact. Their authority is that of antiquity and loose rationalization rather than one of strict logic supported by evidence.

Nor have I any cause to alter the conclusions as to the nature of Chaucer's prosody as outlined in Chapters IV and V; and I now realize that they were outlines. But there is every need to furnish more conclusive evidence than I was able to offer at the time to justify those conclusions. And I should not, as is evident from the foregoing statement about the nature of the prosody of the *ABC* and the *Hous of Fame*, have implied that there was a common basis for all the poems whether they be octosyllabic, decasyllabic, couplets, or in *rime royal*.

I would not be thought dogmatic in my attitude toward final unaccented -*e*, but the deeper I have gone into the MSS. themselves the more support have I found for a firm attitude and no evidence to support a less firm attitude except that of my ear. The testimony of the ear, however, is not reliable evidence for two reasons. The first is that most of us approach unfamiliar poetry with four centuries of verse predominantly five-stress so implanted in our subconscious that we are not free to hear strange rhythms purely.[1] The large amount of rhythmical verse now being written may help correct that condition; but even those poets who are now consciously rhythmical labour under the five-stress subconscious burden. The second reason is that despite the fact that contemporary music has accustomed us to dissonance we still find some of the intervals in the music of Machault in the fourteenth century, for example, strange indeed. They seem awkward and abrupt. The same is true with the poetry of the period. Are we inclined to pronounce an occasional final unaccented -*e* in order to cushion the shock of an effect that is strange although it may be correct? Are we not tempted, for example, as was Robinson in his editing of Chaucer, to pronounce the final *e* of *herte* in such locutions as ' he wold have sen his herte blod ' (' The Complaint of Mars ', l. 124) or ' with herte soore, and ful of besy peyne ' (' The Complaint Unto Pity ', l. 2). As the basis for his text for the ' Mars ' Robinson tells us that ' F [Bodleian Fairfax 16] therefore because of its general conformity to the spelling

---

[1] Spenser thought that he was capturing Chaucer's rhythm in the September Eclogue of *The Shepheards Calendar* where the verse is predominantly four-stress with only an occasional five-stress line.

of the best MSS. of other pieces, has been used as the basis of the
present edition' (*Chaucer's Complete Works*, p. 1,035). And of the
text of 'Pity', he remarks of the MSS., 'the spelling of all is very
bad, and is normalized in the present text. A number of verbal
corrections have also been accepted . . .' (p. 1,035). But what was
Robinson's basis for thinking that the spelling was very bad?
Merely, that the spelling of the MSS. did not permit the reader to
read the poem as an iambic decasyllabic poem? But what is the
testimony of Bodl. Fairfax 16, admittedly a good MS.? Line 124
of 'Mars' reads 'ffor sorow he wolde/have sene his hert blode;'
and for l. 2 of Pity, (titled 'Balade' in the MS.) 'with herte soore / and
ful of besy peyne.' If the reader pays attention to the virga both
readings of the MS. are satisfactory:

$$
\begin{array}{c|ccc|cc|cc|cc}
2 & 4 & 3 & 3 & 2 & 2 & 3 & 2 & 2 & 1 \\
\end{array}
$$

ffor sor-ow he wolde have sene his hert blode

$$
\begin{array}{c|c|c|c|cc|cc|c}
2 & 3 & 2 & 2 & 3 & 2 & 2 & 1 & 1 \\
\end{array}
$$

with hert sore and ful of be-sy peyne [1]

I shall have occasion to discuss several of these instances where at
first I was inclined to sound the -*e*.

Of one thing I have become more firmly convinced than ever.
It is useless to attempt to develop or substantiate a theory of prosody
on anything but the manuscripts themselves. Although Xerox
copies made from microfilms of the original manuscripts, and the
microfilms themselves are useful and often necessary, they are by no
means infallible. Many of the notations so valuable for substantiation
of a theory simply do not reproduce. This is true, for example, of
Bodl. Fairfax 3. In the microfilm the marks are faint but clear. In
the Xerox copies they are invisible.

Early investigators of Middle English prosody ignored for the
most part the marks of punctuation that appear in the manuscripts.
They ignored them because they did not understand them. In Early
Middle English the marks are fairly consistent in their meaning.
The clerical-scribes understood the intonational significance of these
marks. When lay-scribes began to produce manuscripts one can
detect a gradual degeneration in the understanding of their original
significance and substitutions began to appear, until by about 1415

[1] The pitch intonation notation.

the marks tend to disappear altogether. It is not by chance that some of the later MSS. of Lydgate, a monk, are among the few where their original significance was preserved. I am indebted to Professor Rudolph Willard for pointing the way that has resulted in the present essay.

It was he who called my attention to the work of Mr. Peter Clemoes on the ecclesiastical origins of the marks of punctuation. I had made my own investigation of the *cursus* before reading the work of Margaret Schlauch and Margery Morgan. Since their studies are easily available I have thought it unnecessary to include all of the details of my own work on the subject. I am also indebted to those Chaucerians who have been incapable of believing in the fallibility of scholars such as Child, Ellis, Skeat, and that host of Teutonic scholars, a group notorious for building elaborate structures on unsubstantiated hypotheses. Their reluctance critically to examine these earlier hypotheses has made me anxious not to repeat their mistakes of hasty generalization.

I am deeply grateful to the Research Foundation of the University of Toledo for grants for basic materials and for substantial aid in matters relative to publication. I also wish to thank Mr. Wallace Martin for reading proof.

Chapter I

ECCLESIASTICAL AND SECULAR INFLUENCES: RHYTHM, INTONATION, AND PUNCTUATION

BEFORE turning our attention to Chaucer's prosody I think it would be useful to restate certain truisms about poetry that, just because they are truisms, one is apt to overlook. We must also examine in some detail the nature of the rhythms in the 14 C. with which Chaucer would be familiar. Fortunately several able scholars have concerned themselves with this matter and we need only review their achievements.

The critic of a poem must, I think, first attempt to recreate it in his mind and spirit; only then has he a right to analyze it. For a full understanding of it, he must not only think of it as an integrated work of art—i.e., as an object with significant form—but he must also see it in relation to the tradition of poetry to which it belongs, as a monument reflecting the social and linguistic conditions of that age, and as a vitalizing and altering factor in that tradition. In all ages, sensitive critics like Aristotle, Longinus, Dante, Gascoigne, Dryden, Pope, Wordsworth, Coleridge, Pound, Eliot, and MacLeish, to name but a few, have recognized the necessity for such an approach, which one may formulate as follows: (1) A poet's immediate popularity will be in direct ratio to the closeness of his techniques to those of the prevailing tradition. (2) His vocabulary, however overlaid with ' poetic diction ', will be essentially the vocabulary of the audience to which he addresses himself. (3) Within certain limits he must catch in his verses the rhythms of contemporary speech of the tongue in which he is writing. (4) A contemporary disciple of a poet is expected to have and probably does have a clear understanding of the basic characteristics of the work of his master. No less a poet than Robert Bridges, certainly an authority on prosody, amplifies point three. He writes (*Milton's Prosody*, Oxford, 1921): ' Just as quantitative verse has its quantitative prosody, so syllabic verse has its syllabic prosody, and accentual verse will have its accentual prosody. *All three are equally dealing with speech-rhythm*, and they all approach it differently, and thus obtain different effects. It might be possible perhaps, and it

B

is certainly conceivable, to base the whole art of versification on speech-rhythm, and differentiate the prosodies secondarily by their various qualities of effect upon the speech ' (pp. 110, 111). Bridges also points out that ' Skeat's (VI, lxxxv) statement that Chaucer "is so far from conforming to the uniform type of line that he usually does his best to avoid it; and the more skilfully he does this, the more he is appreciated for his variety " . . . is very strange if set beside Professor Skeat's usual method of scanning Chaucer's verses; indeed the two are irreconcilable.' (p. 119). It is easy to trace in the work of the mid-century poets of today the influences of older poets such as Eliot, Williams, Marianne Moore, Frost and others. What is true of poets today has always been true of poets. And I am certain that Hoccleve who acknowledged Chaucer as his master had a clearer understanding of Chaucer's prosody than did Tyrwhitt, Child, Skeat, or Ten Brink.

The great number of Chaucer MSS., as well as statements by his contemporaries, attest to Chaucer's early and continuing popularity. We must concede, therefore, that his prosodic innovations were not such as would strike his listeners as strange. They were easily acceptable. He was capturing the rhythms, the intonations, and the stresses to which their ears were adjusted. In fact, they would have been aware of the intonations of their language which we have only recently begun to recover. Had he used an archaic pronunciation, as Skeat first suggested, he would have revealed an eccentricity incompatible with the way of great poets or of men prominent in economic and political life, and Chaucer was both. No person was less eccentric than he. Even Child, one of the earliest and most influential investigators of Chaucer's pronunciation and the person most responsible for the sounding of final *e*'s, would have rejected the idea of his archaism. He found the sounding of so many final *e*'s ' puerile ' and productive of ' a monotony all but intolerable ', but his concern was not with language and verse that was ' most agreeable but what was the actual rule of our language at the end of the fourteenth century '. He thought, as did Tyrwhitt, that final unaccented -*e* was just beginning to disappear at the end of the fourteenth century. Richard Weymouth, who fought for the tradition of Chaucer's prosody held by Gascoigne, Spenser, Dryden, Pope, Coleridge, and others, believed that the final -*e* had begun to disappear in the twelfth century and that the process was completed by the time Chaucer began to write. Today scholars largely accept this latter view.[1] Child believed, too, that the 'Summoner's Tale' was 'to all intents and purposes a drama', that its characters were 'perfectly distinguished and self-distinguished'. Not only the lady, but the impertinent squire, the lord, and everybody were 'made to present themselves'. He found the friar 'as masterly as Falstaff' and he could see no difference in the way the two were created. He thought, moreover, that Chaucer and Shakespeare had 'the same faults occasionally' in that Chaucer made 'the Pardoner talk of himself as only another person would' and as Shakespeare made Richard III (*The Scholar Friend*, 1952, p. 23). The foregoing statement shows conclusively that Child thought that he was discovering the speech rhythms in use by Chaucer and his contemporaries. It was my contention in *Verses of Cadence* (Oxford, 1954) that Chaucer worked in and modified the English tradition, and caught in his rhythms the speech rhythms of the highly cultivated audience for which he wrote.

What was the nature of these speech rhythms? In a valuable preliminary study on the 'Liturgical Influence on Punctuation in Late Old English and Early Middle English Manuscripts' (Cambridge, 1952), Mr. Peter Clemoes reminds us of what many may have overlooked. In Old English times 'all education was under monastic control before the rise of the Universities. Liturgical practice affected any kind of writing intended to be read aloud; and reading aloud was the normal practice both in public and private' (p. 7). Even after the rise of the Universities in the Middle Ages with the advent of the Dominicans, Franciscans, Carmelites in the thirteenth century, and the Benedictines a little later, the religious influence was dominant. We have only to recall the names

[1] This matter of final -e has posed many problems for the historical grammarian. Joseph and Elizabeth Mary Wright (*An Elementary Middle English Grammar*, Oxford, 1923), for example, were aware that final -e in words of English origin 'continued to be written long after it had ceased to be pronounced,' and that 'in the Midland dialects it had ceased to be pronounced in all forms by about the middle of the fourteenth century' (p. 69).' They recognized, too, that the final -e in words borrowed from the French had disappeared earlier than in words of English origin; they spoke of Chaucer as being 'behind the spoken language of his time' (pp. 102, 103). They could, therefore, only account for Chaucer's possible pronunciation by insisting that 'he was a conservative poet', although adding that '*his metrical forms are no sure guarantee of how he* actually pronounced such forms in his spoken language' (p. 70). From my own studies under Mrs. Wright and with conversations with Professor Wright, I know that they never permitted themselves any *literary* or *stylistic* pronouncements. That they would accept the current hypothesis about Chaucer's poetry formulated by British, German, and British scholars with the resulting necessity of postulating the pronunciation of final -e is not surprising. The important thing is that they were skeptical of Chaucer's use of final -e *in his spoken language*.

of Roger Bacon, Duns Scotus, and Wycliffe at Oxford to be fully
aware of this influence.

The liturgical influence was evident in the effect on *rhythm*,
intonation, and *prosody*. It is important that we consider each.

In spite of mounting evidence afforded by an examination of the
spelling of the MSS. themselves, of the colloquial nature of much
of Chaucer's language, of the significance of the marks of punctuation, of the meaning of verses of cadence (which I shall discuss
in this essay), of the influence of dictamen on Chaucer's prose
rhythms, of the nature of French, Italian, and English verse in the
fourteenth century, of the impossibility of thinking of the single
verse as the unit of measurement, many scholars have been reluctant
to abandon the idea of a prosody for Chaucer based on regularly
alternating stressed and unstressed syllables. They speak of his
infinite variety and read him aloud with a monotonous drone that
denies the presence of variety. Manly, after finishing his monu-
mental labours, realized that Chaucer's verse did not possess the
regularity that previous investigators had assumed for it, and he
thought a complete re-examination was in order. Useful as the
iambic-decasyllabic theory may have proved itself as a stimulant to
Chaucerian studies, one must not forget that it remains an unproved
hypothesis. Since Ellis's *On Early English Pronunciation* (1867–1888),
it has been widely held as proved and therefore regarded as a law.
It has become a Procrustes bed.

In the present chapter, instead of postulating a theory of prosody
for Chaucer and then trying to make the evidence fit, let us examine
as dispassionately as possible the various facets of the evidence and
then see if by imaginative insight we can make a synthesis that
exceeds ' the common mathematics of literary research ', and results
in a theory of prosody that satisfies the four requirements for a good
poet.

Since Chaucer's popularity necessitates the assumption that his
technique was not far from that of the prevailing tradition, some
understanding of the prevailing tradition is important. In Italian,
French, and English the hemistich had been popular. Of the three
traditions only the French was strictly decasyllabic, and none had
the pattern of regular alternation of stresses. It was, therefore, as
I have pointed out, essentially a rhythmic rather than a metrical
line (*Verses of Cadence*, pp. 33–54). Skeat was aware that the iambic
pentameter line was un-English and a meter of which no English

poet before Chaucer 'had ever dreamt' (Skeat, Works, III, 383). He explained the iambic pentameter line by analogy with Machault; but unfortunately Machault never wrote iambic pentameter and his analogy collapses. (See *Verses of Cadence*, pp. 43–44.)

Skeat revealed a remarkable agility in his explanation of Chaucer's *rime royal* stanza. Although finding Chaucer 'indebted in the first instance to French poets ', he ' conformed his lines, as regarded their cadence and general laws, to those of Boccaccio and Dante '. And again: 'the idea of the heroic couplet was also, I suppose, taken from the French . . . but here, again, Chaucer's melody has rather the Italian than the French character ' (III, xliv). But what of the Italian line of Dante? Professor Levi (*Della Versificazione*, Genoa, 1931, Quoted in *Verses of Cadence*, p. 39) points out that there are 828 variations possible in the line.

Gone is the time when scholars can taken an attitude toward the spelling of the MSS. such as that taken by Ten Brink (*Chaucer's Sprache and Verskunst*, 1884): ' It goes without saying that MS. forms which the evidence of rime and metre proves to be incompatible with Chaucer's phonetic system have been removed and replaced by more appropriate ones ' (English translation, p. 33). Ten Brink would not tolerate anapestic or trochaic rhythms (§300, p. 209), and where they occurred he would emend the text. Manly, after years of careful scrutiny of the extant Chaucer MSS., came to have a respect for the scribes that early investigators did not have. My own examination of the principal MSS. clearly reveals that not a single one can be read as iambic pentameter without frequent emendations. Far too many Chaucerian studies have been based on an acceptance of a theory of prosody as proved, whereas no theory has yet been proved. The currently held theory, like the one I am proposing, is, as I have said, an hypothesis. Manly made no attempt to list the variations in the MSS. in the matter of final -*e*. His text is, therefore, not the ideal monument for the study of the prosody. Sir William McCormick told Manly that he would perform a greater service to scholarship were he to give accurate texts of two or three of the best MSS.

I am constantly surprised at the unwillingness of many contemporary scholars to entertain the thought that possibly these early investigators were wrong. I am even more surprised that they refuse to re-read critically these earlier studies. It is possible, of course, that most scholars derived their knowledge of Child's

'Observations' from Ellis's inclusion of the substance of the
'Observations' in Part I of his *On Early English Pronunciation*, from
which scholars would be unable to check the faulty hypotheses on
which Child worked. This willingness of scholars to accept the
work of earlier scholars without checking the original sources
produces many errors. As Whitehead observed, however, 'the
scandal is how unhesitatingly later thinkers have accepted their
conclusions without pausing to re-examine them in terms of changed
[scholarly] conditions'. (*Dialogues* (Mentor), p. 110.)

Chaucer did speak of his 'verses of cadence', however, and his
meaning has puzzled scholars. Margery Morgan ('A Treatise on
Cadence', *MLR*, XLVII, 156–164 *passim*) has discussed the possible
meanings of 'cadence' and found it 'tempting to assume' that it
could refer 'to a whole stylistic manner'. She linked 'cadence' to
'cursus' and 'rhythmical *clausulae*' and was aware of the importance
of the MS. punctuation for a proper understanding of the requisite
intonation. She developed her thesis with scholarly modesty,
pointed out the rhetorical function of the marks of punctuation (to
indicate intonation) and concluded with the suggestion that
'rhythmic pattern, indeed might well be regarded as the dominant
feature of such prose, a feature which rhyme, balance, and other
rhetorical devices merely served to emphasize; and "cadence" a
term denoting rhythmical *clausulae*, often rhyming, would readily
have been extended, in general use, to refer to the whole practice of
this later rhetoric' (p. 164). I agree with Miss Morgan and I hope
to show the strict meaning of 'verses of cadence', as referred to
by Chaucer, and further suggest how the rhythms of cadence
eventually influenced his later work, by not binding himself to a
fixed succession of feet—in other words, that he wrote rhythms
rather than meter. In the course of this chapter, I shall explain why.

The patterns of the rhythms could stem from two main sources:
from the Latin of Cicero and from the native English colloquial
rhythms. Cicero's influence could come directly from the orations
and letters, or indirectly from the orations and letters through the
Papal Chancery, eventually into the Liturgy, and finally, into the
more formal style of secular prose. Before proceeding with a detailed examination of the effects of the liturgy on rhythm, it is first
necessary to understand the differences between *rhythm* and *meter*.

According to Quintilian (*Institutio Oratoria*, IX, IV, 46–51 *passim*,
Loeb trans.) 'rhythm consists of certain lengths of time, while

meter is determined by the order in which these lengths are arranged'.
He recognizes four principal types of rhythm: *dactyllic* (one long
syllable balanced by two short, ♩♪♪), *paeonic* (one long followed
by three short, the three short receiving the value of the long,

♩ ♪♪♪), the *iambic* (a short followed by a long, ♪ ♩), and the
choreus (frequently called the *trochee*, a long followed by a short,
♩♪).

Although the foregoing were also employed in meter, there was
an important difference. In rhythm it '*does not matter* whether the
two shorts of the *dactyl* precede or follow the long; for rhythm
merely takes into account the measurement of the time; that is to
say, it insists on the time taken from its rise to its fall being the
same. '. It would be well, I think, for those who insist on the
classical terms for meter to heed Quintilian's next statement. ' The
measure of verse on the other hand is quite different; the *anapest*
(˘˘ –), or *spondee* (– –) *cannot be substituted* at will for the *dactyl*, nor
is it a matter of indifference whether the *paeon* begins or ends with
short syllables. Further, the laws of meter *not merely refuse* the
substitution of one foot for another, but *will not even admit* the arbitrary substitution of any *dactyl or spondee* for any other *dactyl or
spondee*. For example, in the line

Panditur interea domus omnipotentis Olympi

the alteration of the order of the *dactyls* would destroy the verse.
Another important difference is ' that rhythm has unlimited space
over which it may range, whereas the spaces of meter are confined,
and that, whereas meter has certain definite cadences, rhythm may
run on as it commenced until it reaches the point . . . of transition
to another type of rhythm '. He speaks, too, of the greater number
of rests and the greater license of disposing of these rests in rhythm
than in meter.

But how is this relevant to our discussion? It is simply that in
Cicero's speeches the most important part of the sentence was the
end—the *clausula* ' where the rhythm becomes most palpable '—and
here he used definite rhythmical patterns. These patterns for quantitative prose were adapted in the Middle Ages for a patterned
accentual prose which influenced the vernacular rhythms.

Professor Th. Zielinski (*Das Clauselgesitz in Cicero's Reden*, rev.
by A. C. Clark, *Classical Review*, XIX, 164–172 *passim*) pointed out

that an extended examination of 17,902 *clausulae* in Ciceros speeches supports the rules for the *clausula* which he was able to deduce. His theory was that every *clausula* had two parts, a basis, and a cadence. ' The basis ', to quote Clark, ' consists of a *cretic*, or its metrical equivalent, the cadence varies in length, and is trochaic in character ', generally from two to five syllables. The following are the three forms of Class I.

$$(1) \; — \; \smile \; — \; | \; — \; —$$
$$(2) \; — \; — \; — \; | \; — \; — \; | \; \smile$$
$$(3) \; — \; — \; — \; | \; — \; \smile \; | \; — \; \smile$$

An important distinction exists between Form and Type. The Type is fixed by the *caesura*, which may be after the first, second, third, or fourth syllable; or, but this is rare, the whole *clausula* may consist of one word without *caesura*. Examples of the Types are : (α) *indicaretur*, (β) *non oportere*, (γ) *morte vicistis*, (δ) *civitas possit*, and (ε) *restituti sint*.

Class II permits of slight license (a) two shorts ($\smile \; \smile$) can replace any long($—$) syllable.

Form I. $— \; \smile \; — \; — \; \smile$

In *făcĕrĕ cō netur*, for example, the two shorts of *făcĕ-* are equivalent to the *in-* of *indicaretur*; in *ēssĕ vĭdĕ atur*, the shorts of *vĭdĕ-* are equivalent to the second long in *nōn ŏpōrtērĕ*; in *cōmmĕdī cădĕre*, the two shorts of *cădĕ*—are equivalent to the third long in *nōn ŏpōrtērĕ*. A combination is also possible, as in *făcĕrĕ pŏtŭīstī*, etc.

A second license is that an *epitriton* may substitute for the *cretic* in the base; the weak form ($— \; \smile \; —$) being replaced by a *choriambic* ($— \; \smile \; \smile \; —$), the strong form ($— \; — \; —$) by a $— \; \smile \; — \; —$.

The Ciceronian rhythms are uniform throughout his writings with the exception of the letters to Atticus, which depend on accent rather than quantity. Many of the letters *al Familiares* are, however, just *as metrical* as his speeches. Whereas foreigners and barbarians found it difficult to master the quantity of Latin vowels, the mastery of Latin accent was very simple. The chief point being, as Clark pointed out, that words in which the penultimate is long are paroxytone (e.g., *perfrégit*) and those in which it is short are proparoxytone (e.g., *víncula*). Strange scansions began to appear in such writers as the Spanish Juvencus (*c.* 330) and the Syrian Commodianus (*c.* 233). The metrical prose of St. Cyprian, Symmachus, and Sidonius gave way to accentual or rhythmical prose. In various writers of the last half of the fourth century one finds a mixture of meter and rhythm. St. Ambrose (c. 340–397), St. Jerome (331–420), St. Augustine (340–430), and the Sermons of Leo I (Pope 450 A.D.) are rhythmical. The prose of Boethius is a *cursus mixtus*, although he was capable of both methods. The Letters of Gregory the Great (540–604) mark the full development of the mixed style. The experts in the prose rhythms felt that rhythm in prose fell into abeyance after this, although Clark believed that it must have lingered in some places, as at Monte Cassino, from which it was revived 400 years later.

The Ciceronian rhythms began to re-emerge in the eleventh century in the work of Alberic of Monte Cassino, John of Gaeta, into the twelfth century, and thence into the composition of Papal letters, and the system known as *Cursus Curiae Romanae*, based *not* on meter but on accent.[1]

The orthodox *stylus Gregorianus* came into universal use in ecclesiastical documents and occasionally in non-ecclesiastical literature. We find it, for example, in Papal Bulls, letters, privileges, dispensations, indulgences, and communications; in sermons, prayers, collects, chants, and graces; in the Policraticus of John of Salisbury (1110–1180), the writings of St. Thomas Aquinas (1225–1274), and in the correspondence of Heloise and Abelard. The use of the *cursus* began to decline under Nicholas IV (1288–1292), disappeared from Bulls in the fourteenth century, but survived in literature in the Latin works of Dante (1265–1321), the letters of Petrarch (1304–1374), and *de Mulieribus Claris* of Boccaccio (Clark, 'The Cursus, etc.', pp. 17–19).

When Renaissance scholars discovered the meaning of quantity they avoided the use of any of the prescribed phrases. They abandoned the use of the *cursus*; but its influence did not stop, because the ears of worshippers were constantly bombarded with its rhythms. The collects and other prayers of the church were, as I. Shelly reminds us ('Rhythmical Prose in Latin and English', *The Church Quarterly*, LXXIV), composed rhythmically, 'not in verse but with accented cadences corresponding to the most part to Cicero's favourite metrical endings' (p. 89). Anyone listening to the offices of the church would have constantly heard the use of the *clausulae*.

[1] I have taken my facts about the *cursus* from J. L. Poole, *The Papal Chancery*, 1951, and from two papers by A. C. Clark: 'The Cursus in Medieval and Vulgar Latin,' 1910, and 'Prose Rhythms in English,' 1913.

To the men of the Renaissance, the style of the Collects and the liturgical forms of the Missal and Breviary seemed barbarous, yet the stress of the accents and the fall of the cadences must have continued to impress themselves on the ears and minds of those who heard them day by day (*Ibid.*, p. 91).

The Ciceronian influence, as I have mentioned, is that of the colloquial style of his letters to Atticus, however, rather than that of his more formal other writings. These exhibit metrical *clausulae* characteristic of his other work, only here they appear to be accentual. The accentual cursus did not develop from a misunderstanding of the ancient system such as I have outlined, but it reflected an historical development. John of Gaeta made no vital changes except that of limitations. Known in the thirteenth century as *artificiosa dictionum structura, cursus* is one particular feature in *Dictamen* or the *Ars Dictandi.* Grammar taught the correct use of words in phrases and sentences; Dictamen dealt with the rules of composition for letters in a formal and ornamental style. At first the rules did not necessarily involve the question of rhythm, but once the system of *cursus* reached its full development, it did. *Dictamen* was looked upon in the fourteenth century as 'neither altogether prose nor altogether metrical, but participated in both' (Quoted in Poole, p. 78). The terminology belongs to a time when for ordinary purposes accent had superseded quantity and a man writing hexameters, for example, made changes in the meaning of the traditional names of metrical feet. Every dissyllable is a *spondee*; every trisyllable of which the penultima is unaccented is a *dactyl*. *Mare*, for example, ranks as a *spondee* rather than as a *trochee* (or Quintilian's *choreus*); *dominus* as a *dactyl* rather than as a *cretic*. The rules concern only the closing phrases, the rules for which were fixed and precise:

1. Cursus Planus: dactyl+spondee /◡◡ | //
2. Cursus Tardus: dactyl+dactyl /◡◡ | /◡◡
3. Cursus Velox: dactyl—two spondees /◡◡ | ////

The rigidity of the rules deprived the *cursus* of the variety and flexibility it possessed in early times. No other caesura was possible than that prescribed for each of the three endings. Occasionally, however, certain licenses gained admission; these were invariably ' accentual representatives of the ancient forms when the *cretic* was resolved ' (*Ibid.*, pp. 79–93 *passim*).

We could simplify the foregoing for practical purposes by

thinking of the *planus* as consisting of five syllables with accents on the first and fourth, e.g. *vóces testántur*, English equivalent, *sérvants depárted*; of the *tardus* of six syllables with accents on the first and fourth, e.g. *méa curátio*, English equivalent, *pérfect felícity*; and of the *velox* of seven syllables with accents on first and sixth, and a minor on the fourth, e.g. *gáudia perveníre*, English equivalent, *glórious ùndertáking*.

The important thing about the development of the medieval *cursus* is that it was no more a question of the combination of single words than it was in ancient times: ' it is the combination of syllables which make up the close of a rhetorical period, the Clausula Rhetorica ' (*Ibid.*, p. 93). The key lies in the *cretic* which from Cicero's time constituted one of the two schemes for ending a phrase, the other being the ditrocheus (— ◡ — ◡). We must realize, as I have already pointed out, that the accentual *dactyl* originates in the metrical *cretic*, and that the accentual *spondee* comes from a metrical *trochee*. The Clausula Rhetorica consists of a cretic base followed by a *trochee*, a *cretic*, or a double *trochee*. Although thirteenth century writers of *Dictamen* attempted to construct precise rules for the terminations appropriate to the comma, colon, and period, writers only agreed that the sentence should end with a *cursus velox*.

Although the foregoing discussion of the *cursus* applied only to its use in the Papal Chancery, the *cursus*, as I have mentioned, served many other liturgical uses, in the Breviary, for example, and the Missal. These, in turn, influenced the rhythm of the Collects in the Prayer Book. Shelly has pointed out that in the Prayer Book of 1549, in the Sunday and Holy-Day Collects, of the 187 endings of clauses, at least 94 are in a form of *cursus*. We have, for example, the following:

Cursus planus: Márty̆r Săint Stéphĕn, hélp ănd dĕfénd ŭs, práy'rs ŏf thy péoplĕ.

Cursus tardus: Thém thăt bĕ pénĭtĕnt; hánd ŏf thy májĕsty̆; góvĕrn'd ănd sánctĭfíed.

Cursus velox: Ríse tŏ thĕ lífe ĭmmórtăl; péoplĕ whĭch cáll ŭpón thĕe; désire ŏf thy̆ húmblĕ sérvănts.

Cursus planus (answering to Cicero's éssĕ vĭdĕātŭr): Wríttĕn fŏr oŭr léarnĭng; mány̆ ănd gréat dángĕrs; háppĕn tŏ thĕ bódy̆

If this situation exists in English of the sixteenth century, how much more likely would it be to find it in the literature of the fourteenth. And we do.

It is pertinent to ask to what extent the rhythms discussed in the foregoing find their way into English prose of the fourteenth century and specifically, in the works of Chaucer and others. And do these ryhthms find their way into his poetry?

Before pursuing this investigation, however, we must distinguish between the rhythm of the *cursus* and the native English rhythms. The differences are obviously those which arise from the differences in vocabulary. Latin is essentially a polysyllabic language, whereas most native words in English are disyllables and monosyllables. Clark pointed out, however, that there is a striking similarity in the two in that the 'trochaic cadence' is 'a characteristic of both languages. This was modified in Latin by the *cretic* base which precedes the *trochaic* movement and the use of harsher measures in the middle of the clauses. The *trochaic* rhythm is chiefly found in the *clausula*, and does not generally extend further than over a few syllables. In English the *trochaic* movement pervades the whole sentence and frequently produces the effect of blank verse ' (Clark, 'Prose Rhythm, etc.', p. 18). Saintsbury also somewhere speaks of the trochaic 'hum' of English. A large portion of medieval lyrics, especially those based on Latin models, are certainly trochaic. Although the three forms of *cursus* came into English from the Latin and from the Romance Languages, the naturalization of these words effected an alteration in the cadences. Illustrations of this abound in the Collects. Of the ninety-five cases, for example, which do not belong to forms of the *cursus*, no less than seventy-one end with an accented syllable, e.g. *ármoŭr ŏf líght, contémpt ŏf thy̆ wórd* (Shelly, pp. 81–98 *passim*). This is wholly alien to Latin where the accent is never on the last syllable of a word, and where writers carefully avoided ending a sentence on an accented monosyllable, unless they sought a bizarre effect as Horace occasionally did. Rhythms ending in an accented syllable are essentially native rhythms. The rhythms of such *clausulae* as *cóvĕr thĕ eárth* and *cóme tŏ thy̆ líght*, both of which end in a stressed monosyllable are not Latin in character. The clash and fusion of Latin and native rhythms are often the occasion of some of the more striking effects in English. The rhythms of ' The Miller's Tale ' are strongly English.

Margaret Schlauch (' Chaucer's Prose Rhythms ', *PMLA*, LXV, June, 1950, 4:568–589) discusses the effect of the *cursus* on Chaucer's prose rhythms. Sections I–IV of her essay present a scholarly, condensed, and much fuller account of the medieval aspects of the *cursus* than I have done. In the application of her findings to Chaucer's prose, however, I think she goes too far; and to his poetry, not far enough.

She elevates the artistry of prose above that of poetry by stating that the ' obvious meters of verse require much less awareness ' than mature prose rhythms. ' Obvious ' is a question-begging word, and she erred in using it about Chaucer's verse. Good poetry, as has been recognized since classic times, must be as carefully written as good prose. She might have learned from Coleridge what Coleridge learned in his school days at Christ's Hospital from the Rev. James Bowyer, ' that poetry, even that of the loftiest, and seemingly, that of the wildest odes, had a logic of its own as severe as that of science, and more difficult, because more subtle, more complex, and dependent on more and more fugitive causes. In the truly great poets . . . there is a reason assignable not only for every word, but for the position of every word ' (*Biog. Lit.*, London, 1891, p. 3). Or, as Coleridge later realized, ' there is no profession on earth which requires an attention so early, so long, or so unremitting, as that of poetry ' (*Ibid.*, p. 23), a statement expanded in his famous definition of a poet (*Ibid.*, pp. 150, 151–end of chapter 14). He was fully aware, however, that in his own day, and this was even more true later in the century, except for such experimenters as Hopkins, that whereas ' in the days of Chaucer and Gower, our language might . . . be compared to a wilderness of vocal reeds, from which the favourites only of Pan or Apollo could construct even the rude Syrinx; and from this the constructors alone could elicit strains of music ', the language of his own day had been ' mechanized . . . into a barrel organ ', as a result of which ' literature at present demands the least talent or information ' (*Ibid.*, pp. 18, 19). The poets of his own day were, too, seekers after ' striking images ', but in their ' diction and metre ' they were ' comparatively careless ' (*Ibid.*, p. 157).

Coleridge's insistence on the arduous nature of the poet's calling was not peculiar to him, but has been stressed by critics from Longinus and Quintilian to Ezra Pound, and is the very essence of the ' new criticism '. In times of poetic dearth—and the latter half of the nineteenth century, particularly in America, was such a period —poets tend to forget this. A good poet, however, is constantly experimenting with and extending the potentialities of his prosody. This has been true in all ages. A. C. Clark (*The Cursus*, etc.), for example, in speaking of the Greek hexameter mentions that after Homer it began to tend more and more to the *dactylic*—' the luxuriance of Homer gradually dies out and finally in Nonnus (*c.* 500 A.D.) we find that 25,000 verses yield only nine types of hexameter. Child reduced the 282 variations of the *endecasyllables* to one, as did Ten Brink with the 'heroic' line. The poet is not only careful in the arrangement of the selected sounds, such as alliteration, assonance, rhyme, and vowel gradations, but he strives to give a unique rhythm to each sentence by the manipulation of these sounds in order to convey his feelings toward his subject. The syntactical pattern and the structure of the imagery are likewise important. My quarrel with those who adhere to an over-simplified prosody for Chaucer is that they obscure the superb rhythmical effects that Chaucer achieves. They talk about them, but these effects never appear in their oral reading of him.

Schlauch traces the development of prose rhythms, explains and richly illustrates the various types of *cursus* that she finds in Chaucer's prose, and provides the reader who has not pursued his own independent studies with an admirably condensed picture of the subject. The fact that we disagree about final -*e* makes little difference. I would classify certain locutions differently than she does, but the disagreement is one of detail, therefore, and not of principle. I believe that any person anxious to understand Chaucer's prosody should read her discussion of the *cursus*.

I take strong issue with her on three points in Section Five of her article. She accepts two hypotheses that are wholly unwarranted. She accepts, for example, Joseph Bihl's analysis of Chaucer's verse rhythms with his belief that 'the generally unambiguous accentuation of verse lines permits us to observe that stress was in a state of flux in Chaucer's time, so that he was free to treat many dissyllables, for instance, as either iambs or trochees'. There is no evidence in Bihl (*Die Wirkungen des Rhythmus in der Sprache von Chaucer und Gower*, Heidelberg, 1916) that he verified the hypotheses of the prosody on which he erected his elaborate structure. He accepts Ten Brink and the iambic theory. 'Unambiguous' is one of the things that, I hope to show, Chaucer's verse is not. Teutonic scholarship is unfortunately loaded with studies carefully erected on unsubstantiated hypotheses. The necessity for so many shifts in stress should have laid open to question the iambic theory of prosody. Chaucer was not capricious in his use of accents. It is my strong conviction after working with Chaucer MSS. for several years that this idea of the stress-flux is a crutch for the iambic deca-syllabic theory, but a paper crutch capable of supporting nothing.

The second point of disagreement concerns final -e. Recognizing that linguistic evidence is against the sounding of final -e before consonants as well as vowels, for consistency's sake she accepts it as sounded. Since, as I have pointed out (' Chaucer's Final -E in Rhyme ', *PMLA*, LXII, 910–935), that, even assuming that the iambic-decasyllabic theory was correct, that final -e never occurs at the end of line in circumstances where we might assume that for metrical purposes it was sounded within the line, that it was not pronounced in lyrics based upon known Latin models, and was not pronounced in London speech, I think she wrongly classifies her evidence.

Furthermore, what basis does she have for her statement that ' prose discourse *must surely* have been ahead of *more conservative poetic usage* '? What is the evidence that Chaucer's usage was con-servative? If an adaptation, or subtle transference of the freedom allowed by the *cursus* and its adaptation to suit the genius of native English speech, into a verse of a surprisingly subtle but moderately regular versification is to be conservative, then Chaucer was con-servative. I choose a different term to describe Chaucer's achieve-ment.

Allowing for the foregoing disagreement in the matter of hypo-theses, her presentation of her evidence in Section VI for Chaucer's use of the cursus is a masterful handling of the common mathe-matics of scholarship. Even if we eliminate the many questionable examples based on the assumption that final -e was sounded, she still lists abundant examples from Chaucer's prose (pp. 584–589), and has effectively demonstrated his practice. Her conclusions are convincing and she leaves no possibility of doubt that ' Chaucer's prose has been influenced by the long tradition of cadenced medieval Latin prose '. She is aware that Chaucer may have acquired forms unawares, that ' he may have picked up the patterns by ear ', that he may have studied them, or that he ' may have become aware of them in the official letters and formularies which employed them by prescription '. She recognized, too, that Chaucer adapted the traditional forms to English usage, and that he showed a remarkable freedom, independence, and subtlety in varying them. With all of this I most heartily agree. But if this is true of his practice in his prose, should we not also expect the same in his poetry, if as Bridges has pointed out any form of prosody—quantitative, syllabic, and accentual—deals with speech-rhythms?

Charles E. Shain in his ' Pulpit Rhetoric in Three Canterbury Tales ' (*Modern Langauge Notes*, LXX, No. 4, April 1955, pp. 235–245) shows Chaucer's intimate knowledge of the *artes praedicandi* in the Pardoner's, Summoner's and Merchant's Tales and suggests that echoes also occur in the speech of the Wife of Bath, who spent so much of her time listening to sermons. We might expect to find the *cursus* in the *Monk's Tale*, and *Prioress' Tale*, and we do. A casual examination reveals the *tardus*: *soveryn conquerour* (M. 2095), *lucre of vileyne* (Pr. 491); *planus: doon in hire childhede* (Pr. 501), *kut to my semynge* (Pr. 648); *planus* (Cicero's *esse videatur*): *pitous lamentacion* (Pr. 621); *velox: reverence of Christes moder* (Pr. 539). He also makes frequent use of an irregular cursus consisting of a spondee (or trochee) and a dactyl: *artow Sathanas* (M. 2003), *out of miserie* (M. 2006), *which that thou art falle* (M. 2006), *fynger wroght was he* (M. 2008), *laude and heighe renoun* (M. 2096).

Since the rhythms of English often end on a stressed syllable, the classical type of *cursus* was not possible. Chaucer did, however, modify the classical types to fit the English. This is what one expects a poet to do. Chaucer knew when to use such rhythms and when not. Dorothy Everett ('Chaucer's "Good Ear",' *RES*, XXIII (1947), 201–208) has cited many impressive examples of Chaucer's excellent ear, even showing how he can use the alliterative verse to superb effect. He shows it too in the way he uses unsubtle verse for an unsubtle subject. The opening of the Reeve's Tale is as unsubtle in its rhythms as verse can well be. So, too, is the Miller's. They have a strong regularly *iambic* tone. In the passages of conversation, however, Chaucer catches the rhythms of colloquial speech:

> And she sproong / as a colt dooth in the trave
> And with her heed / she wryed faste awey
> She seyde I wol not kisse thee by my fey
> Why lat be quod [she][1] / lat be nicholas
> Or I wol crye / out harrow and allas
> Do wey youre handes / for youre curteisye
>
> (Hengwrt 3282–3287)

These rhythms have a strong English cast.

But Chaucer does not limit his use of the classic *cursus* to those

---

[1] Both the Ellesmere and Hengwrt have *ich*, which is an obvious error.

tales told by the persons in holy orders. Many examples of the *cursus planus* occur in the ' Prologue ': *seken straunge strondes* (13) and *ful of fresh floures* (90); the *tardus*: *half cours yronne* (3). If we only casually examine the *Hous of Fame* we can easily accumulate an overwhelming number of examples of the *cursus*. We have the following within the opening lines:

Planus (/ × × / ×)
    why these oracles (11)
    of these miracles (12)
    neyther the distaunce (18)
    more then that cause is (20)
    folkys complexions (21)
    (Nyl) as now make mensyon (56)

Tardus (/ × × / × ×)
    is an avision (7)   and dawn cupido (137)
    (I wol) make invocacion (67) (His) blynde sone, and
    (with) special devocion (68)   Vulcano (138)
    (mal)icious entencion (93)

Trochaicus (/ × / ×)
(That alwey for to) slepe her wone is (76)

Fully to understand the prosody of a poet, however, it is necessary to study his practices from his earliest to his latest efforts. The great ease of Chaucer's most mature work resulted only from long practice and discipline. No one explanation will account for all the facets of Chaucer's prosody, because he undoubtedly extended his experiments gradually. Did we know the chronology of his work we could proceed more intelligently with his prosody. As it is, his prosody, rightly understood, affords us an important tool with which to date his work. The rhythms of the ' Prologue ', however, and a scansion of the first fifteen lines reveals not more than two lines that are identical.

Or take the word *felicity* as listed in the *Concordance*. Out of sixteen citations of the word from the poetry, one of them is a *cursus planus*: *felicitee parfit* (A. Prol. 338) and nine are the *cursus tardus*:

(/ × × / × ×)   after felicitee   A. Kn. 1266
                    and in felicitee   B. Mk. 3467
                    in heigh felicitee   C. Pard. 787
                    in moore felicitee E. Cl. 109

C

parfit felicitee	E. Mch. 1642
so great felicitee	E. Mch. 1675
of pleyn felicitee	ABC 13
and in felicite	T. C. 4480
and his felicite	LGW. 1588

I shall later have much more to say of Chaucer's use of the *cursus* or cadence. First, however, we must consider the matter of intonation, closely related to it.

Incidentally, the *cursus planus* occurs frequently, too, in *Piers Plowman*. In a selection from Passus VI (B-Text) we find such expressions as *with our longe fyngres* (10), *cherches to honoure* (12), and *hede how his leggeth* (15). We find the same rhythms in *Havelock the Dane*: *wodes and wonges* (397) and *Helfled the tother*.

I am not, of course, suggesting that Chaucer, or that the authors of *Piers Plowman* and *Havelock the Dane* were consciously using the *cursus planus* but that this rhythm was widely enough disseminated in the prose that the poets found it natural to use it in their own work. But since so much of Chaucer's poetry is direct discourse, we should not expect nearly so conscious a use of the *cursus* as in his formal prose. Only as those patterns had subtly impressed themselves through the liturgy on the speech patterns would they echo in the poetry.

The nature of Chaucer's subject matter calls for the familiar style, at times for the colloquial. Every sensitive reader of Chaucer has long been aware of the colloquial quality of his verse. In ' Chaucer's Colloquial English: Its Structural Traits ' (*PMLA*, LXVII (December, 1952), 7:1103–1116) Schlauch has analyzed the traits by which ' Chaucer gains his effect of unstilted ease, of fluency and unpretentiousness throughout all of his work, and how the passages in particular achieve their air of lively verisimilitude '. Schlauch says nothing about a change of attitude toward final unaccented -*e*. Colloquial structure calls for the colloquial pronunciation. It is inconceivable that a poet of Chaucer's urbanity would, for the sake of a fixed metric, alter the colloquial stress or pronunciation of a word. To read Chaucer's lines as iambic lines necessitates such an alteration. My whole investigation of the basis for Chaucer's prosody was to find a prosody that supports the qualities Schlauch finds in the poetry. Chaucer knew what people actually say in the midst of life. Like every dramatic poet he had tuned his ear to the impromptu and deliberate speech of people living their lives. He absorbed the stream of human speech in all its random disorder and by practice and discipline created pseudo-utterances that he manipulated in writing, in the strict and purposeful structure of structures that make up a poem.

The source for colloquial English is, of course, in the English of centuries' standing enriched and altered by the influx of words and rhythm differing in texture from the native. Chaucer was at least bilingual and undoubtedly spoke Central French. He would not have exchanged the native intonation for a word because of the prosodic requirements. No good poet ever does that.

The rhythm of Chaucer's verse must, therefore, reflect the degrees of informal speech of the various characters—of the Cook as well as of the Knight, of the Wife of Bath as well as of the Prioress or Cressida, of the Squire and Troilus as well as of the Monk and the Pardoner. These rhythms will be the native rhythms variously affected by the liturgy and by other formal locutions. They will be heightened pseudo-utterances that capture the qualities—rhythm, intonation, vocabulary, and structures—of real utterances.

What Quintilian said about the rhythm of Latin verse applies equally well to English verse. It is the approximately equal time between stresses that is important. If we are to use classical terms we must use them as they were used for *rhythm* and not as they were used for *meter*. I prefer, however, a different notation. Mr. William Thompson (*The Rhythms of Speech*, 1924) in his scholarly analysis of the temporal aspects of rhythm demonstrated that English verse is largely in 3/8 time, with variations in 2/8 time and others. My own studies in *More Modern American Poets* demonstrated that Thompson's statements apply to modern poetry as well. Professor Kenneth L. Pike lends support to this position in his statement that in English the rhythm ' units tend to follow one another in such a way that the lapse of time between the beginning of their prominent syllables is somewhat uniform ' and points out that ' the recurrent stress timing is perhaps even more important than the number of syllables in iambic or trochaic groups or the like ' (*The Intonations of American Speech*, 1949, p. 34). Armstrong and Ward (*A Handbook of English Intonation*, 1931) take a similar position—that taken by Quintilian: ' In each sense group the stressed syllables occur at more or less regular intervals of time, and the unstressed syllables, whether many or few, occupy the time between the stresses . . . such regularity is not monotonous, however, because of the pauses that are made between groups and the varying intonation of the groups ' (p. 7).

Thompson was aware of the importance of *intonation* in poetry but made no attempt to provide an accurate notation. Since *intonation* is important, let us glance briefly at some statements of British and American scholars about its nature. Armstrong and Ward support Thompson, although they do not specifically mention 3/8 time. Let me quote from *A Handbook of English Intonation*. ' By intonation we mean the rise and fall of the pitch of the voice when we speak. . . . Intonation varies from locality to locality and from individual to individual ', and I might add, from period to period. But these variations ' are not essential for correct and good English speech, and their absence would not be missed by anyone who had not made a special study of intonation ' (p. 1). Or, as Kenneth Pike has pointed out, ' all speakers of a language use basic pitch sequences in similar ways under similar circumstances; . . . these abstracted characteristic sentence melodies are known as intonation contours. . . . One sentence may have several contours, and a single contour may have several meaningful parts ' (p. 20). Actually, of course, the *cursus* is a speech contour of a definite intonational pattern.

Intonation should not be confused with *stress*, although there is a connection between them. Stress is ' the breath force we use when speaking. In a sentence those words are said to be stressed which are pronounced with greater breath force than the others. These are the words felt by the speaker to be important ' (A & W, p. 8). The modern scholar of prosody, for example, is not interested in superimposing on a line of verse a pattern that violates the rhetorical significance of a line. He stresses the word or words that embody the idea or ideas. In the opening three words of *Lycidas*, for example, he stresses all three—' yet ', ' once ', and ' more '. In addition, however, he alters the pitch of these words to set each off from its neighbours. This alteration in pitch is *intonation*. Many American scholars treat pitch, stress, and juncture all as parts of intonation.

The pitches of intonation are relative, and as Professor Pike is careful to explain, their significance ' is determined by their height *relative* to one another ' (Pike p. 25). English, moreover, has two basic tunes in intonation. In Tune I, ' the stressed syllables form a descending scale. Within the last stressed syllable, the pitch of the voice falls to a low level ' (A & W, p. 4). As Armstrong and Ward remind us, ' it is the correct relative pitch of these unstressed syllables which is most essential. The pitch of the unstressed syllables occurring between the stresses matters little, so long as it is not far removed from that of the previously stressed syllable '. Many variations between stresses are possible, but ' the pitch of final unstressed syllables is most important. These must be either on a low level, which is the most usual, or must begin very low and descend a little lower '. In Tune II, ' the outline of the first tune is followed until the last stressed syllable is reached. This is on a low note, and any syllables that follow, rise from this point. If the last stressed syllable is final, the rise, which is an essential of this tune, occurs within the stressed syllable itself ' (*Ibid.*, p. 6).

Even more important for our purpose is the general nature of liturgical rhythm. The following statement on rhythm from the *Liber Usualis*, edited by the Benedictines of Solemnes (Tournier, Belgium, 1947) is the ultimate authority on the complicated subject of Gregorian chant: ' It is in the well-ordered succession of such movements that rhythm essentially consists. In its elementary form, the rise or *arsis* is the beginning of the rhythm unit or movement; the fall or *thesis* its end. The rhythmic fall or *thesis* will necessarily occur on every second or third note in the course of the melody —like the fall in every second or third syllable of the words which accompany it. Hence the impossibility of two such falls occurring in immediate succession, unless, of course, the first be a note of double value. But notice carefully that these steps or falls form in an ascending movement the *arsic* part, or rise, of the larger rhythm, just as every step one takes in climbing up a hill goes to the general movement upward. This whole movement upward is known as the *arsic* part of the larger rhythm. Similarly when the movement is downward, every rhythmic rise or *arsis* of the voice forms a part of the larger rhythm, just as in walking down a hill the regularly uplifted foot is part of the downward movement. This whole movement downward is known as the *thesic* part of the larger rhythm ' (xxvi, xxvii).

This rhetorical speech stemming from Gregorian chant was ' in essence a development of the intonation of [a] normal speech . . . used in addressing a large gathering of people in the open air, where there is a tendency to keep the voice on one note, but to allow it to drop at the end of the sentence '. This tendency was systematized ' for the reading of the Gospels, Lessons, and Epistles, for the formal utterance of prayers, Collects and Blessings, and in the simpler

service of the Office, for the chanting of Psalms ' (Clemoes, p. 7).
Since the texts were non-metrical, with accents at irregular intervals,
the phraseological divisions were those of tradition: the *commata*, or
shortest division of a rhetorical period; the *cola*, a portion of the
sentence intermediate between *comma* and *periodus*; and *periodus*, a
complete sentence.   Quintilian (ix, iv, 123–125 (Loeb, III, 577))
defines these terms as follows:

Commata [or comma]—' an expression of thought lacking
rhythmical completeness' and may 'consist of a single word'
(p. 122).

Colon—' the expression of a thought which is rhythmically
complete, but is meaningless if detached from the whole body of
the sentence ' (p. 123).

' Both the *commata* and *cola* are fragmentary and require a con-
clusion ' (p. 124).

Periodus—' It has two forms.   The one is simple, and consists of
one thought expressed in a number of words, duly rounded to a
close.   The other consists of *commata and cola*, comprising a number
of different thoughts. . . .   The period must have at least two *cola*.
The average number would appear to be *four*, but it often contains
even more (p. 125).   To read the cadences correctly, the liturgical
reader needed a special kind of punctuation.

Mr. Clemoes has traced the evolution of this special kind of
punctuation from its continental origins in the 6C to its English
forms in the 13C and 14C.   These symbols, known as *positurae*, can
be briefly summarized. The *punctus circumflexus* indicated a drop in the
voice (Tune I) and a *punctus elevatus* signified a rise in the voice
(Tune II); and the *punctus versus* signified the lowering of the voice
at the end of the period (again Tune I), and the *punctus interrogativus*
the inflection of an interrogative sentence (again Tune II).[1]   Mr.
Clemoes has shown us the use of *positurae* in Aelfric's homiletic prose,
in the Orrmulum (13C), in Wycliffe (14C), in Trevisa and others.

Originally the use of the positurae in MSS. from the 12C to the
14C reveal that the scribe employed a *punctus circumflexus* to indicate
a drop in the voice (Tune I) before ' and ' connecting two parts of

---

[1] Cn the musical staff we could represent the *punctus circumflexus* as the interval from
g down to e; the *punctus elevatus*, g-f-e-g; the *punctus versus*, b-a-b-e (the e being a fifth
below b); the *punctus interrogativus*, g-f-e-f-g. The symbol for the *punctus versus* is our
modern semicolon (;) and that for the *punctus elevatus* is an inverted semicolon (⁏). This
latter is the most important mark of punctuation in the MSS. By the time of Chaucer
the symbol for the *punctus circumflexus* had become debased   It and the *punctus versus* had
become the same symbol, a low *punctum* (.).

a sentence and a *punctus elevatus* to indicate a rise in the voice (Tune II) at a suspension in the sense, appropriate, for example, ' between a subordinate and main clause in a complex sentence; between a relative and a main clause, and after a participial construction, or a vocative which is not final '. Three of these forms survive in modern chant. (See *The Liber Usalis*. Edited by the Benedictines of Solesmes, 1947, pp. xx, xxi.) But as other influences begin to appear we must not expect to find so regular a use of the *positurae*.

As secular influences began to exert themselves, for example, both in prose and poetry, and the centre of gravity shifted away from the liturgy, we still find *positurae* being used, but not in the strictly formal way of the earlier period. A general debasement has taken place and several *positurae* are used interchangeably, and modifications occur. Instead of the strict notation for a *punctus elevatus* (√), we have two debased forms—the *colon* (:) and what we might call the double podatus (√). These and the *virga* (/) indicate a rise in the voice or Tune II. Certain scribes use the *punctum* (·) when placed above the line. The scribe of Oxford Bdl. Douce 158, for example, generally used a very light *virga*, but occasionally a high *punctum*, as in ' Than is he next · to his overthrowing ' (*Reg. of Princes*, l. 65). Instead of the strict forms for the *punctus circum-flexus* (?) and punctus versus(;) we have the low *punctum* (.). By the 12C the *punctum* indicating the *punctus versus* is followed by a capital, whereas the *punctum* indicating the *punctus circumflexus* is followed by a lower case letter, both, however, Tune I.

Before concentrating our attention on the marks of punctuation in the Chaucer MSS., let us briefly examine those marks in the MSS. of his predecessors and contemporaries. MS. Cotton Caligula Aix is a 14C compendium of English and French works. The following passage from Layamon's *Brut* represents the conservative and litur-gical punctuation: ' King ich þe wulle telle √ for serlai þe spellen. mi fader coman þe king √ luuede me þurh all þing. þa war þich on beame √ wunder ane fif(?) þa ich wes as noȝe √ fifteen ȝere ' (f92ᵛ).

A French poem, *The Life of St. Josaphaȝ* in octosyllabics, follows. The marks of punctuation are √ and . at the ends of the lines. There is no regular alternation. It has a sing-song quality and the √ definitely marks a rise in the voice. In *The Owl and the Nightingale* which follows, the only mark is a high *punctum* (·) at the end of line. The one exception, :, is not sufficient for generalization: the

hyeþ þey wurse : flesch þe gost ·

In the French tale that follows (ff. 249–259) the √ and the . alternate fairly regularly—the √ following the first rhyme word of the couplet: *-age* √ *-ysage, guyse* √ *-emprise.*

In Robert of Gloucester's *Chronicle* (Cotton MS. Caligula Axi) the scribe uses the high *punctum* as follows:

> Sir Edward and sir henri · and sir vinfray de boun.
>
> To gloucestre hii wente · to enfermi þen toun
>
> þs ha begonne mid hor ost · fourten niht abide.
>
> þe erl of glousetre was · in the forest biside.
>
> and sir jon Gyfard al so ·

In Harl. 3724, an early MS., the marks of ' Pater noster in anglico ' occur at the end of the line: a low *punctum* alternating with √ or in an occasional instance with ; :

> þat holi lyed þat laste ay √
>
> þu send his ous þis ilka day.
>
> fforgiue ous alle þat we hauiþ don
>
> Als we forgiuet uch oþir may.
>
> Ye lete us fatte ȳ no sondinge;
>
> Als fealde us fra þe soule þȳge may

Many readers may be inclined to minimize the importance of the foregoing discussion for an understanding of Chaucer's prosody. I, however, think it is highly important. It should help the reader better to understand the milieu in which Chaucer was working. Instead of being a sport detached from the tradition of the poetry and prose of his day I think that, like Shakespeare, he accepted the tradition, but like every original poet altered it and brought it to a pitch of perfection that his followers could not sustain. They were fully aware of what he was doing but lacked the uniqueness of vision that enabled him to make the perfect fusion of thought and form. If we are aware of his milieu we can better see him in the act of fashioning his instrument that will serve his purposes so beautifully in *Troilus and Criseyde* and the *Canterbury Tales.* The road to that achievement was a long one.

Chapter II

CHAUCER AND HIS CONTEMPORARIES

IN the light of what we have discovered about the significance of the marks of punctuation, let us now turn our attention to the application, we might almost say survival, of those marks in the works of Chaucer and his contemporaries. And let us begin with *Piers Plowman*.

The marks of punctuation in the MSS. of *Piers Plowman* differ widely. The later the MS. the less clear the significance of the marks, if any. The conservative practice is evident in MS. Camb. Univ. Ffl 1–6:

> Conscience and þe kinges √ yn to courte wente
> Where houlde an hundryd √ yn houes of selke
> Servauntys hyt semed √ þat seruyd atte barre
> To plede for penyys and poundys the lawe
> And nat for loue of our lord √ unlouse here lippys onys
> þowe myȝtyst betere mete þe myst √ on maluerne hillys
> þene gete a mon of here mouth √ tyl money wer y shewed
> þene ren þer a route √ of ratonys as hyt were
> And smale mys wyth hem √ þen a þousend
> Comen to the cõsayl √ ffor here comen profyt
>   CC Passus I: 158–167

The voice would tend to rise in the arsis to the √ and then to fall in the thesis. Modern linguistic scholars would, I believe, think of the √ as indicating a single-bar juncture necessitating a slight pause at this point. A single-bar juncture, according to Paul Roberts (*Understanding English*, New York, 1958) ' can occur only between primary stresses, and it consists of a lengthening out of the phonemes before the break with a sustension of the pitch level across the break ' (251). I shall later have more to say about this, but I should caution the reader that although we shall find the lengthening out and the sustension, we shall not invariably find that the virga appears between primary stresses.

An examination of eleven MSS. of John Gower's *Confessio Amantis* throws light on the deterioration of understanding about the marks of punctuation. The handwriting of Bodleian Fairfax 3 is obviously early. The scribe uses the punctus elevatus (√) and the low punctum (.) with their customary significance—the first, a rise in the voice; the latter a fall. The mark is faint in the microfilm, fails to reproduce in a Xerox copy, and for a really detailed careful study demands the MS. itself. In Book I, the *punctus elevatus* occurs at the end of lines 1, 2, 4, 6, 7, 10, 15, and 16. The first low punctum falls at the end of line 17. A more typical use of the two marks occurs at I: 197–202 or I: 209–221. Here is the first selection:

> O Genius myn oghne clerk√
> Com forþ and hier þis mannes schrifte√
> Quod Venus þa. and I uplifte√
> Min hefd wiþ þat. and gan beholde√
> The selve Prest which as sche wolde √
> Was redy þere, and sette him doun
> To hiere my confessioun.

The scribe of Harleian 3869 makes a freer use of the *punctus circumflexus* but less seldom one of the *punctus elevatus*. A typical example of his practice is that found in I: 132–142:

> O Venus, queene of loves cure
> Thou lif . þou lust . þ ou mannes hele
> Behold my cause and my querele
> And ȝif me som part of þi grace
> So þat I may finde in þis place
> If þou be gracious or non
> And with þat word . I sawh anon√
> The kynge of love and qweene boþe
> Bot he þat kyng wiþ yhen wroþe√
> His chiere aweiward fro me Caste .
> And forþ he passede ate laste

In both illustrations the marks are essentially intonational guides. Since normally the voice would fall at the end of the line, the *punctus circumflexus* warns the reader not to let his voice fall. In the MSS. which from the nature of their handwriting are obviously later—Camb. Univ. DdVIII. lg, Camb. Univ. M1L. 21, Pembroke Coll. 87, Bodleian MS. Arch. Selden. B11, Bodleian Hatton 51, and others—there are no marks at all. In St. John's College MS. B.g, an obviously late MS., a high *punctum* at the end of every line has little if any significance. And the Chaucer MSS.? Oxford Bodleian Fairfax 16 throws interesting light on some of the earlier poems. In 'Complaynt of Mars and Venus', for example, the scribe begins

with a high *punctum* (·), uses it throughout the first 15 stanzas,
then changes to a virga (/). Quite obviously they mean the same
thing. B. M. Harleian 2392 which is a good text, but one which
will be important evidence for a rhythmical rather than a metrical
prosody uses only the virga (/). Hengwrt and Ellesmere both use
the virga (/), but the Ellesmere makes further use of two marks
which are important: one from the point of view of intonation, the
other from the point of view of the treatment of the end of the line.
The first (✓)[1] is definitely a question mark. If carefully observed it
will indicate a different reading from that suggested by the punctuation of modern editors. The second (✓) indicates that, contrary
to the usual practice, the person reading aloud should be careful
not to let his voice fall at the end of the line but should suspend it
into the next line. Interestingly enough, this mark occurs chiefly in
fragment E.

As a rule there is no end punctuation in MSS. of this period.
Where the MSS. do have an end mark it is a low punctum (.),
which is a debasement of ,[2] a mark which occurs at the end of every
line in Hoccleve's *De Regimine Principum*, Bodleian Ashmole 40.
In this same MS., the scribe begins with *punctus elevatus* (✓) but
changes to a virga (/) at line 10. It is evident from the interchanges
that (✓), (/), and (·) mean the same thing.

It becomes apparent as one examines the various MSS. of this
period that the scribes no longer understood the full significance of
these marks. In Gower's *Confessio Amantis*, Bodleian Fairfax 3,
for example, the mark (✓), used as a question mark in the Ellesmere, does not indicate a question. The scribe of Bodl. Fairfax 3
also occasionally uses a high punctum (·) for his inner punctuation.

By ignoring the internal marks of punctuation and blindly
accepting the tentative hypothesis that Chaucer used the Italian
endecasyllabo, Child, totally without an understanding of the subtlety
of that line, was able to put forth the idea of the iambic quality of
Chaucer's verse, an idea that with slight modifications has become
universally accepted. We must remember, moreover, that Child
had access to no Chaucer MSS. and worked from a very corrupt
printed text. Although it was recognized by him that there were
exceptions to his theory on every page, he clung to his theory. It
is true that if the reader neglects the evidence that the marks of

---

[1] The actual mark in Ellesmere is less angular than the *punctus elevatus*, the forerunner
of the virga.
[2] See footnote 1 page 75.

punctuation offer for a theory different from that of the iambic decasyllabic theory, he can find that by far the majority of the lines in the MSS. can be so scanned. But what of those that cannot be so scanned? What if there are no final -*e*'s in the MS. to eke out such a scansion. Robinson, as I have already pointed out, attributes their absence to carelessness in spelling. But is it? Where an admittedly good MS. from a textual point of view omits so many of the final -*e*'s that appear in other MSS. is it not likely that they were not pronounced?

One Chaucerian has remarked to me that at the close of the 14C. language was changing so rapidly that a poet writing in 1410, say, would not have understood the prosody of a poet writing in 1398 or 1400. This remark was to explain the difference between the prosody of Hoccleve and Chaucer. Anyone with a grain of linguistic sense knows that language does not change so rapidly. And since Hoccleve was a supposed student or disciple of Chaucer and knew him personally, is it likely that he did not understand Chaucer's prosody? I shall have more to say about Hoccleve's prosody in another chapter.

In the matter of the pronunciation or non-pronunciation of final -*e*, however, what would have been the position of one of Chaucer's contemporaries who undertook to read his poems to an audience? Would he, for example, when reading from the Campsall MS. of *Troilus* pronounce all the final *e*'s that need pronouncing for the iambic decasyllabic theory and when reading from BM. Harleian 2392 of *Troilus* supply all the missing *e*'s in order to make this theory tenable? Not likely! My guess would be that Harleian 2392 would more accurately reflect the pronunciation than would the Campsall. And what does a modern reader do when he reads Robinson and then turns to Manly, Root, or Donaldson? Is he consistently inconsistent?

In *Troilus and Criseyde*, for example, Robinson writes *speche-seche-eche* (I, 702, 4, 5); *stynte-answerde-entente-ferde-yerde* (I, 736–740); *geste-leste* (II, 83, 4); *telle-helle* (II, 104, 5); *chiere-matere-yfere* (II, 149, 151, 2); *seye, tweye* and many others. In Harleian 2392, we have *spech-sech-ech, stynt, answerd, entent, ferd, yerd, gest, lest, tell, hell, chier, matier, infier, say, tway, hour, devour, clere, fair, deer, debonair, repair*, etc., etc.

Far more significant than the spelling of Harleian 2392, however, is the difference in the text. The important thing is that whereas Harleian 2392 cannot possibly be read metrically, it reads rhythmically exactly as does Campsall, or any of the others. But what is the prosodic system that I propose for Chaucer? If we ignore the obvious fact that he wrote in octosyllabic and decasyllabic couplets and in the rime royal stanza, and concentrate on the inner structure of the verse we shall find several styles. Even a rather cursory analysis reveals that he wrote *verses of cadence* in *A devoute balette to our ladye* (ABC), a rather simple but effective rhythmical verse in the *Boke of the Duches*, a modified verse in the *Hous of Fame* in which *verses of cadence* play an important part, a very colloquial conversational verse in *Troilus and Criseyde*, and finally the infinitely subtle verse of the *Legende of Good Women* and the *Canterbury Tales*.

The whole matter of Chaucer's prosody has been unduly simplified because of the general acceptance of the iambic theory of his versification. It is not my intention to attempt a thorough analysis of the various types of Chaucer's prosody, but I am anxious to show that the superficial classification of his work into iambic octosyllabic couplets, iambic decasyllabic couplets, iambic quatrains with alternating rhyme, and rime royal stanzas obscures both the nature of his achievement and his development. It is not the external appearance of his verse that matters but rather the internal structure of his verse—his rhythms. When I spoke of the *Troilus* and the *Canterbury Tales* as being written in *cadence* I was wrong although it is clear that *cadence* played an important part. I was not wrong, however, in my suggestion as to the nature of the verse in these poems. But what I discovered about the internal quality of his rhythms in those poems has led me by a circuitous route to what I think Chaucer really meant when he spoke of his verses of cadence.

Let us look first, therefore at *A devoute balette* [ABC] which scholars have agreed was one of Chaucer's earliest works, and *it is* certainly one of his earliest decasyllabic poems. For the purposes of our discussion I shall accept their dating although a more thorough investigation of the poems in the light of my findings may raise some questions. I am not concerned with statements within the poems that might fix the limits of the date of their composition, but solely with the movement or nature of the verse itself.

Since Chaucer speaks in the *Hous of Fame* of his *verses of cadence*, we should seek the meaning of the term in poems antedating it. And *A devoute balette* [ABC] is acknowledged as being such a poem. If the reader forgets the old rules for final -*e* he will find that every

line is decasyllabic, and follows the hemistich tradition of being
divided by the virga into arsis and thesis. I like to think of the two
parts of the line receiving approximately the same time in reading.
Let the reader read to an imaginary metronome with one beat for
each part of the line and I think he will hear the music. Instead of
analyzing the entire poem, let us confine our attention to the first
twenty-four verses. The following are the verses as found in Bodleian MS. Fairfax 16:

Almyghty / and alle mercyable quene   1
To whom al this worlde / fleeth for socour
To have relees of synne / sorowe of teene
Gloriouse virgyne / of all floures flour
To thee I flee / confounded in errour   5
Help and releve / thow myghty debonayre
Have mercy / of my perilouse langour
Vanquysshed hath me / my cruel adversayre

Bonte so fix / hath in thine hert his tent
That wol I wote / thow wolte my socour bee   10
Thow kanst not werne hym / that with good entent
Axeth thyn helpe / thyn herte is ay so free
Thow art largesse / of pleyn felicitee
Havene of refute / of queyte and of reste
Loo how that theves seven / chacen me   15
Helpe lady bryght / er that my shippe to breste

Comfort ys noon / but in yow lady dere
ffor loo my synne / and my confusion
Which ought not / in thy presence apperre
Han take on me / a grevouse accion   20
Of verray ryght / and disperacion
And as by ryght / they myghten wol sustene
That I were worthy / my dampnacion
No mercy of yow / blysful hevenes quene

An analysis reveals the following examples of the classic
cursus planus (/ × × / ×)

fleeth for socour	(2)
(con)founded in errour	(5)
(of my) perilouse langour	(7)

tardus[1] (| × × | × ×)

of pleyn felicitee	(13)
and my confusion	(18)
and disperacion	(21)

tardus[2] (| | | × ×́)

(my) cruel adversayre	(8)
(thow) wolt my socour be	(10)
that with good entent	(11)
(a) grevouse accion	(20)
(my) damnacion	(23)

The remaining fifteen lines, ending as they do on a stressed syllable are essentially native English, but they are examples of *cursus* nonetheless. We are concerned with the rhythm of that part of the verse following the virga.

Line 1 depends for its subtle effect on the intonation the reader gives it. Essentially it is a slightly modified tardus: *alle mercy able quene—| × × | × |*. Line 16 has the same rhythm (*or that my shippe to breste*). We have a modified *planus* (| × × |) in lines 3 (*sorowe of teene*), 4 (*all floures flour*), 6 (based on Cicero's *esse videatur*) (*myghty debonayre*), and 24 (*hevenes quene*). Line 9 is modified *tardus* (| × × | × |) (*hath in thin hert his tent*); so, too, are lines 12 and 14: (| | × ×̀ × |) (*thyn herte is ay so free*) (*of queyte and of reste*). Line 15 is a *trochaicus* (*theves seven chacen me*). Line 17 is a modified *tardus* (| × | | × |) (*but in yow lady dere*); and 19 another variation on the same (| × | × × |) (*in thy presence appere*); so, too, is 22 (| | × | × |) (*they myghten wol sustene*). The rhythms of the foregoing cadences are controlled by the arsic part of the verse. Since every line ends in a *cursus* or *cadence*, isn't this what Chaucer meant by his *verses of cadence*?

I should like to digress at this point and call the reader's attention to the contemporary attitude toward final *-e* as exemplified by the *hert* in line 9 and of *herte* in line 12, the *-e* of *herte* not being sounded because it precedes a word beginning with a vowel. But in ' Balade ' [to Pity], in the same MS., we have the following:

> Pite that I have sought / so yore agoo
> With hert sore / and ful of besy peyne.
> That in this worlde / was never wight so woe
> Withoute dethe /

The pronunciation or non-pronunciation of the scribal final *-e* in such instances as *hert dere*, *hert sore*, or *hert blode* in ' have seen his

hert blode ' (' Complaynt of Mars and Venus ', MS. Fairfax 16) ' my
hert bare of blis ' (' The Complaynt of Analida etc.') or ' my tremblyng hert / so gret gastnesse had ' (Hoccleve, *De Regimine Principun,*
Ashmole 40) inclines me to believe that, even though it seems harsh
to our modern ears, Chaucer did not pronounce the *e* in *herte deere,*
herte made, and elsewhere. I am even more strongly inclined to this
view after examining the first 65 occurrences of heart in the *Canterbury*
Tales as listed in the *Concordance.* Of these 22 were final and undoubtedly not sounded. Eighteen occur before words beginning
before a vowel or h, Child's hypothesis for not sounding the final
-*e*. According to the iambic decasyllabic theory, the remaining 25
would be pronounced. But how does this accord with the position
of the virga in the lines in which these instances occur? Here are
the lines:

With herte pitous / Whan he herde hem speke	(A.953)
Hym thoughte / þat his herte wolde breke	(954)
In to myn herte / that wol my bane be	(1097)
And ever shal / til þat myn herte sterve	(1144)
The deeth he feeleth / thurgh his herte smyte	(1220)
And eck his his herte had compassion	(1770)
And þus with good hope / and with herte blithe	(1878)
His herte blood / hath bathed al his heer	(2006)
And herte soor / and seyde in this manere	(2220)
Myn herte may myne harmes not biwreye	(2229)
That Arcita / me thurgh the herte bere	(2256)
This Emelye with herte debonaire	(2282)
He feeleth / thurgh the herte spoon the prikke	(2606)
His hardy herte / myghte hym helpe naught	(2649)
With herte soor to Theseus paleys	(2695)
Encreeseth at his herte / moore and moore	(2744)
That welled in his herte / syk and soore	(2809)
Gan fallen whan the herte felte deeth	(2804)
Hath in his herte / swich a love langynge	(3349)
Hir thoughte / hir cursed herte brast atwo	(B.697)
The constable / gan aboute his herte colde	(879)
So was hir herte shet / in hir distresse	(1056)
Wepynge for tendrenesse / in herte blithe	(1154)
Of whos vertu / whom he thyn herte lighte	(1661)
The swetnesse / his herte perced so	(1745)

Of the foregoing, in all except two the final *e* would be silent.

In those two, A.2256 and B.879, the pronunciation of the final *e* would certainly seem pleasanter to our ears. But as I have already pointed out, in similar instances in Bodl. Fairfax 16, *hert* is spelled without the final *e*. And as Child warned his readers, it is not what pleases us but what was the actual situation in Chaucer's day.

But to return to the nature of Chaucer's prosody. The date of ' Lack of Steadfastness ', simply called ' Balade ' in Bodleian Fairfax 16, is not known. Every line concludes with a *cadence*. Here is stanza one:

> Some tyme the worlde was / so stedfast and stable
> That mannes worde / was obligation
> And now hyt is so fals / and so disceyvable
> That worde and dede / as in conclusyon
> Ys noo thing lyke / for turned up so don
> Ys alle this worlde / for mede and wilfulnesse
> That alle is loste / for lake of stedfastnesse

$$/ \times \quad \times \quad / \times \quad / \times \times \quad / \times$$
Lines 1 and 3 are *planus* (stedfast and stable, so disceyvable); 2, 4,
$$/ \times \times / \times \times \quad / \quad \times$$
5, 6, and 7 are perfect examples of the *tardus* (was obligation, as in
$$\times \quad / \times \times \quad / \quad \times \times \quad / \quad \times \times \quad / \quad \times \times \quad / \times \times \quad /$$
conclusyon, for turned up so don, for mede and wilfulnesse, for
$$\times \quad \times \quad / \quad \times \quad \times$$
lack of stedfastnesse).

' Merciless Beauty ' is also an example of Chaucer's use of *cadence*. In the first 7 lines, there are three instances of the *tardus* (1, 4, 6), three of the *planus* (2, 3, 7), and one typical English type (5—$/ \times \times \times /$).

But to proceed. Robinson based his text of *The Boke of the Duches* on Bodleian Fairfax 16 but said that ' numerous ungrammatical forms (chiefly bad final *e*'s) have had to be corrected, and the spelling has been normalized to bring it into general conformity with that of the Ellesmere MS. of the *Canterbury Tales* '. By ' having had to be corrected ' Robinson meant that he had to add many final *e*'s . This attitude toward the scribes of the period is presumptuous. The scribes were better educated than most persons of the time and undoubtedly familiar enough with contemporary poetry to know what they were doing. If Chaucer's scrivener Adam was as asseared as many scholars would have the scribes of this period to be things were in a sorry state indeed. A comparison of the pointing between the Ellesmere and the Hengwrt probably gives us the

D

basis of Chaucer's complaint to Adam. I am glad to see, however, that a rapidly increasing body of scholars takes the view that the scribes knew what they were doing.

The opening line of *The Boke of the Duches* illustrates the editorial method. Robinson deletes the *e* of *grete*, probably to make the scansion regular. The MS. reads

> I have grete Wonder / by this lyghte
> How that I lyve / for day ne nyghte
> I may not slepe / wel nygh noght

If the *e* of *grete* was left, then according to the rules formulated by the late 19C scholars, it would have to be sounded. I maintain that one ignores such rules if he understands the prosody. The foregoing lines can be forced into an iambic pattern, or almost.

$$\times \ / \ \times \ / \ \times \ / \ \times \ /$$
> I have gret won der be this lyght

$$\times \ \ / \times \ / \ \ \times \ \ / \ \times \ /$$
> How that I lyve for day ne nyght

$$\times \ / \ \times \ / . \ \times \ / \ \times \ \ /$$
> I may not sle-pe wel nyghe noght

$$\times \ / \ \ \times \ \ / \times \times \ / \times \ /$$
> I have so ma-ny an y-del thoght[1]

The mechanical piano quality of this is deadening. Let us rather heed the internal marks of punctuation, adjusting the intonation to these marks (4 for high level, 1 for the lowest level, and 3 and 2 for the intermediate ones). Although the virga (/) originally meant a rise in the voice, I do not think we should distort the rhythm were one to hold the voice at a level pitch here with a slight pause. In other words, treat the virga as indicating a single-bar juncture.

$$2 \ \ 3 \ \ \ \ 3 \ \ \ \ 3 \ \ 2 \ \ \ \ 3 \ \ 2 \ \ 1$$
$$\times \ / \ \ \ \ / \ \ \ \ / \ \ / \ \ \ \ / \ \ \times \ /$$
> I have grete wonder / be this lyghte

$$2 \ \ \ \ 4 \ 3 \ 2 \ \ \ \ 2 \ \ \ \ 3 \ \ 2 \ \ 3$$
$$/ \ \ \ \ / \times \ / \ \ \ \ / \ \ \ \ / \ \ \times \ /$$
> How that I lyve / for day ne nyghte

$$2 \ \ 4 \ \ \ \ 3 \ \ \ \ 3 \ \ \ \ 3 \ \ 2 \ \ \ \ 1$$
$$\times \ / \ \ \ \ / \ \ \ \ / \ \ \ \ / \ \ \times \ \ \ \ /$$
> I may not slepe / wel nygh noght

$$2 \ \ 3 \ \ \ \ 3 \ \ \ \ 3 \ \ 2 \ \ 2 \ \ 3 \ \ 2 \ \ 1$$
$$\times \ / \ \ \ \ \times \ \ / \times \ \times \ / \ \times \ \ /$$
> I have so ma-ny / an y-del thoght

Perhaps the difference will seem slight, and it certainly is not

---

[1] The intonational patterns will vary slightly from reader to reader, and often quarrel with my own notations.

conclusive.   The unstressed -*ny* of *many* before the virga and the unstressed *an* after the virga is not strictly a single-bar juncture in that they are not stressed, but the pause is possible.   But let us go farther into the poem.

In l. 102 Robinson has emended the text to read

$$\times \quad / \quad \times \quad / \quad \times \ / \qquad \times \ /$$
That no man myghte fynde hir lord

The MS. reads, however,

$$2 \quad 3 \quad 3 \quad\ \ 3 \qquad\ 3 \qquad 2 \ \ 1$$
$$\times \quad / \quad / \quad\ \ / \qquad\ / \qquad \times \ /$$
That no man myght / fynde hir lorde

It does not scan regularly.   Or take line 109,

' Quod she to Juno, hir goddesse ',

as emended by Robinson scans regularly.   The MS. reads

$$4 \quad 3 \quad 3\ 2 \quad 2 \quad 2 \qquad 1$$
' Quod she Juno / hir goddesse '

(l. 109) which does not; but it is satisfactory rhythmically.   Or lines 126, 127:

And she forweped / and for waked
Was wery / and thus the ded slepe

Robinson added final -*e* to *ded* for the sake of smoothness.   Or line 206: Robinson's text reads ' But, goode swete herte, that ye ' whereas the MS. reads 'But good swete herte / that ye . . . ." Instead of being an octosyllablic line it is a six-syllabled one, although it still has four stresses.   In order to make the lines scan regularly as some scholars have insisted they must do, some form of emendation is required in every few lines.

If the reader reads the following passage, making the movement upward in the arsic part to the virga and then lets the voice descend in the thesis, I think he will hear a reading that would be effective when read aloud.   A subtle reader will, of course, achieve a greater variation than would another.   I would suggest the non-pronuncia-tion of the final *e* in *farynge*.

$$4 \quad 3 \quad 2 \quad\ 2\ 2\ 2\ 2 \qquad 1$$
I was war / of a man in blak

$$2 \quad 3 \qquad 3 \quad 3 \qquad 3 \qquad 2 \ \ 1$$
That sete / and had turned his bak

$$2 \quad 2 \ 3 \qquad 2 \quad 3 \qquad 2$$
To an ooke / an huge tree

Lorde thought I who may that be

> What eyleth hym / to sitten here
> Anoon right / I went nere
> Than founde I sitte / even upryght
> A wonder wel / farynge knyght   (445–452)

The absence of a virga in l. 448 suggests a more rapid movement on a more even tone.

Chaucer here makes no use of cadence, and even by paying every possible attention to the original text and by heeding the marks of punctuation the reader senses the lack of any real flexibility in the lines such as we find in the later Chaucer.

This is not to say that the poem lacks charm; and from one point of view the verse is satisfactory. It simply does not permit the psychological subtlety possible in his later verse. In the lover's recollection of his falling in love the verse captures the unadorned simplicity of the occasion. The following text (Bodleian Fairfax 16) differs markedly from the text in Robinson or Donaldson, and the reading permitted by theirs is not possible in this MS. The reader should pay careful attention to the virga (treating it as a single-bar juncture) and to the spelling:

> Amonge these ladyes / thus echon
> Soth to seyn / y sawgh oon
> That was lyke / noon of the route
> ffor I dar swere / withoute doute
> That as the somerys sone bryghte
> Ys fairer clerer / and hath more lyght
> Than any other / planete in hevene
> The moone / or the sterres sevene
> ffor al the worlde / so had she
> Surmonted hem / al of beaute
> Of maner / and of comelynesse
> Of stature / and of so well sette gladnesse
> Of godelyhede / and so wel be sey
> Shortly / what shal y sey
> By god / and by halwes twelve
> Hyt was my swete / ryght al hir selve
> She had so stedfaste / countenaunce
> So noble porte / and meytenaunce
> And love that had wel / herd my mone
> Had espyed me / thus soone

> That she ful sone / in my thoght
> As help me god / so was y kaught
> So sodenly / that I ne toke
> No maner counseyl / but at hir loke
> But at myn hest / for why hir eyen
> So gladly I trow / myn hert seyen
> That purely tho / myn owne thoght
> Seyde it were beter / serve hir for noght
> Than with a nother / to be wel
> And hyt was sothe / for everedel
> I wil a noon /ryght telle the why
> I sawgh hyr daunce / so comelelly
> Carole and synge / so swetly
> Lawghe and pley / so womanly
> And loke / so debonairly
> So goodely speke / and so frendly
> That certes y trowe / that ever more
> Nas seyne / so a blysful a tresore
>
> (816–853)

The absence of many *-e*'s, medial or final, does not permit an iambic rhythm. Chaucer has caught speech rhythms, although simple ones.

When we turn to *The Hous of Fame* in Bodl. Fairfax 16, and read carefully, observing a slight rise in the arsis to the virga and the fall after it, it is possible to find a greater flexibility and a closer approach to the rhythms of speech than was possible in *The Boke of the Duches*. The following passage will illustrate:

> Of Decembre / the tenthe day
> Whan it was nyght / to slepe I lay
> Ryght ther as I was / wonte to done
> And fille on slept / wunder sone
> As he that wery was / for goo
> On pilgrymage / myles two
> To the corseynt / Leonarde
> To make lythe / of that was harde

<pre>
/ × × /   × /   × /
But as I slept / me mette I was
× / × /   × × / ×   /
Withyn a temple / ymade of glas
×   /   / /   / / × ×
In whiche ther were / moo ymages
</pre>
Of golde stondynge / in sondry stages
And moo ryche / tabernacles
And with perre / moo pynacles
And moo curiouse / portreytures
And queynt maner / of figures
Of olde werke / then I saugh ever
ffor certeynly / I nyste never
Wher that I was / but wel nyste I
Hyt was of Venus / redely
The temple / for in portreytoure
I saugh anoon / ryght hir figure
Naked fletynge / in a see.   (111–133)

I have already mentioned the types of punctuation marks that we find in Gower's *Confessio Amantis* which indicate that the prosodic basis is similar to that of Chaucer. Child very early recognized that were one to read Gower's verse as he insisted that one should read Chaucer's the effect would be unbearable. If the reader heeds the meaning of the virga the monotony tends to disappear. A modern silent reader would be more apt to prefer to observe a level tone at the juncture of the arsis and thesis with a slight pause—the single bar juncture (/).

The reader should notice, however, the essential monotony of the verse. The first half of the line moves deliberately; the second half falls away, generally in the intonational pattern 3–2–1, at a quicker pace, like a wave breaking. Does Chaucer make use of the *cursus*? Numerous lines end in a *cursus trochaicus*, such as *swete a steven* (307), *thyng of heven* (308), *hem that feyned* (317), and *hem that peyned* (318). This is an unsubtle locution. Occasionally, the reader runs across a *cursus planus*: *speken of huntyng* (350), but for the most part the lines end in a stressed syllable. This is decidedly beginner's verse; or at least occasional verse written without inspiration. The static position of the virga enhances the wave-like quality. From the point of view of final -*e*'s, both Robinson's and Donaldson's texts differ greatly from Bodleian Fairfax 16 which simply does not permit an iambic reading.

The following passage reveals the danger of oversimplifying the nature of Chaucer's verse. The eagle is talking to Chaucer as he transports him through the air:

> of loves folke / moo tydynges
> Bothe sothe sawes / and leysinges
> And moo loves / newe begonne
> And longe y served / loves wonne
> And moo loves / casuelly
> That betyde / no man note why
> But as a blende man / stert an hare
> And more jolytee / and fare
> While that they fynde / love of stele
> As thinketh him / and over al wele
> Mo discordes / moo jelousies
> Mo murmures / and mo   novelries
> And moo / dissymulacions
> And feyned / reparacions
> And moo berdys / in two oures
> Withoute rasour / or sisoures
> y made / then greyndes be of sondes
> And eke moo holdynge / in hondes
> And also moo / renoveilaunces
> Of olde for leten / acqueyntaunces
> Mo love dayes / and acordes
> Then on instrumentes / be acorded   (675–696)

Only one of the foregoing lines is a purely iambic line, and then not so if the reader heeds the virga (170). Eight of them and in a *cadence* (167, 168, 172, 176, 177, 178, 179, 180). Spondees and trochees are more frequent than iambs.

The text of the *The Parlement of Fowls* in Bodleian Fairfax 16 (there called *The Parlement of Briddes*) differs greatly from those used by Robinson and Donaldson and definitely cannot be made to scan metrically in the way that theirs do. The following few selections show how impossible it is to read the passage metrically. But if one reads them both rhythmically, heeding the significance of the virga, the music is almost the same—certainly there is no sharp distortion:

> Ne wote how he / quyteth folke her hire
> Yet hapeth me in bookes ofte to rede

> Of hys miracles / and of his cruelle yre
> There rede I wel / he wolde be lorde and sire
> > (Bdl. Fairfax 16, ll. 9–11.)

> Ne wot how that he quiteth folk here hyre,
> Yit happeth me ful ofte in bokes reede
> Of his myrakles and his crewel yre.
> There rede I wel he wol be lord and syre
> > (Robinson, ll. 9–11.)

> Of usage / what for luste / what for lore
> On bookes rede I ofte / as I yow tolde
> But why that I speke / al this not yore
> Agon / hit happed me / for to be holde
> Upon a booke was write / wyth lettres olde. . . .
> > (Bodl. Fairfax 16, ll. 15–19.)

> Of usage—what for lust and what for lore—
> On bokes rede I ofte, as I yow tolde.
> But wherfore that I speke al this? Not yoore
> Agon, it happede me for to beholde
> Upon a bok, was write with lettres olde
> > (Robinson, ll. 15–19.)

The reading of lines 17 and 18 in the MS. is better than that in Robinson.

Attention to the placement of the virga in line 226 also gives a different reading from that in Robinson, and a better one.

> I sawgh beaute / withoute any atire
> And yowthe ful of game / and jolyte
> ffool hardynesse flatery / and desire   (225–227)

> I saw Beaute withouten any atyr,
> And Youthe, ful of game and jolyte;
> Foolhardynesse, Flaterye, and Desyr.
> > (Robinson, ll. 225–227.)

In Robinson's version 'jolyte' modifies 'youthe' rather than being a personification as it was undoubtedly supposed to be.

The following two passages further illustrate the divergences in the text.

> Wel bourded quod the duk / by my hatte
> That men shulden alwey / loven causeles

Who kan a reson fynde / or wytte in that
Daunceth he murye / that is murtheles
Who shuld rechche / of that ys rechcheles
Ye quek quod the duk / ful wel and faire
There ben moo sterres god wott / than a paire (589–595)

I wolle noght serv Venus / ne Cipride
ffor soth as yet / by no maner wey
Now syn hyt may / noon other weyes betide
Quod nature / heir ys no more to sey
Than wolde I / that these foules were awey
Eche with hys make / for taryinge lenger here
And seyde hem thus/ as ye shal after heir. (652–658)

Robinson's ' Quod tho Nature ' and ' Quod nature ' if read rhythmically follow the same intonational pattern and take the same time:
♪♪♪♪ . 3 . 3 . 3 . 2 and ♩♪♪ . 3 . 3 . 2. In a cursory examination I have found no certain *cursus*. I can detect, however, rhythmical echoes of the *cursus*, particularly that of the *tardus* (/ / / × ×).
The subtlety arises from a counterpointing of a falling intonation
striking on an accented syllable in such locutions as ' I knowe not
love in dede ' (8), or ' quyteth folke her hire ' (9) ' in bookes ofte to
rede ' (10), and ' and of hys cruelle yre ' (11). This is a subjective
reaction, of course, but it is just such a reaction as Chaucer might
have experienced after abandoning verses of cadence for a different
type of verse.

Actually, of course, the versification of the *Parlement* differs quite
markedly from earlier works of Chaucer. The difference lies not in
its superficial form—the rime royal stanza—but in the internal
structure of the lines. Approaching it with the iambic pentameter
line firmly embedded in one's mind, it can easily be made to fit into
the iambic decasyllabic mold, that is, if one emends the text. But I
think that to regard it as iambic pentameter is to rob it of some of its
subtle effects by confusing the intonational pattern of the line. One
can read some of the poems of a modern poet like Richard Wilbur,
for example, either metrically or rhythmically, but the rhythmical
reading is far more subtle. And since the iambic pattern was not
yet common, or even existent in Chaucer's day, it is not likely that
he was thinking of his lines metrically. What he was doing was
subtly altering the rhythmical tradition and introducing a greater

subtlety into it. Here is the opening of the *Parlement of Briddes*
(Bodl. Fairfax 16).

```
       2   3  2    2      2    3    2 2     2 1
       ×   /  ×    /      /    /    / /     × ×
       The lyf so short / the crafte so longe to lerne
       2   3  2   2        2    3    2   2    2 1
       ×   /  ×   /        /    /    ×   /    × ×
       Thassay so harde / so sharpe the conquerynge
       2   3 2   2      2 3    3    3    2 1
       ×   / ×   /      / /    ×    /    / ×
       The slyder joy / that alwey slyd so yerne
       2   3   2    2   2 2      2     2 2 1
       /   /   ×    ×  × /       /     / / ×
       Al this meene I be love / that my felynge
       2   3   2   2      2   2  3   2   2   1
       ×   /   ×   /      /   ×  /   ×   /   ×
       Astonyeth soo / with a dredeful wurchyng
       2   3   2    2     2   3   2 2   2    1
       /   /   ×    /     /   /  ×   /   ×    /
       So`soore y wys / that whan I on hym thynke
       2   3  2   2    2   3 2   2    2    1
       /   /  ×   /    /   / ×   /    ×    /
       Nat wote I wel wher that I wake or wynke
```

It can, of course, as I have said, be forced into the iambic pattern,
but by doing so we conceal a certain important fact—the manner in
which Chaucer is naturalizing some of the traditional *cadences* into a
decasyllabic prosodic line. What he is doing more nearly approaches
the rhythms of contemporary speech. I mentioned earlier that
there were echoes of cadence in the *Parlement*. The foregoing stanza
is a more explicit example of the presence of cadence. Lines 1 and 2
could be classified as *tardus*; 4 and 6 *planus*; 5 *trochaicus*. Only 7 has
an iambic ending. If we observe the intonational patterns of line 9—
```
       2  3  3    3    3 2   3   2 1                    3  4 3     3
       ' Ne wote how he / quyteth folke hir hire,' line 10—'Yet hapeth / me
       2   3 2 2   2 1              3  3 2     3   2 3       3
       in bookes ofte to rede,' or line 15—' Of usage / what for luste / what
       2   3
       for love,'
```
it becomes obvious I think that Chaucer has achieved a
subtlety that is not evident if we squeeze them into the iambic mold.
Naturally we can find many iambic lines in Chaucer. English with
its many monosyllabic determiners, connectives, and nouns just
naturally falls into iambic or trochaic patterns, but to say that
Chaucer was consciously conforming his verse to a rigidly iambic
pattern is quite a different matter. In the first three stanzas, if one
carefully heeds the rhetorical implication of the line. I have found no

wholly iambic pattern. The important thing is that Chaucer, beginning with a rather stiff, regular syllabic versification, strongly under the French influence in the *Boke of the Duches*, and passing through the conscious stage of writing cadences is gradually achieving an ease and fluidity which will eventually enable him to do with verse the same that Shakespeare did—be the master and not the servant. Chaucer's achievement in the *Pardoner's Tale* is comparable to Shakespeare's achievement in the great tragedies. Scholars, by lumping all of Chaucer into the iambic hopper have been able only indistinctly to perceive this. That this is true is evident whenever a Chaucerian scholar reads Chaucer's verse publicly—an agonizing experience for the listener with any sensitivity for English rhythms.

In *The Legend of Good Women*, Chaucer achieves greater flexibility, a characteristic of his later work. The opening lines capture the typical wave-like quality of English speech. I would not labour the point or wish to overstress it, but there is less tendency to make the two parts of the line as balanced in syllables as before, although the time division remains about the same. If the first part of the line is crowded, the second is more deliberate, and vice versa. At least so I hear the following:

> A thousand tymes / I have herd telle
> Ther ys joy in hevene / and peyne in helle
> And I acord wel/that it ys so
> But netheles yet / wot I wel also
> That ther is noon duelling / in this contree
> That eythir hath in hevene / or in helle y be
> Ne may of hit / noon other weyes witen
> but as he hath herd seyde / or founde it writen
> for by assay / ther may no man it preve
> But god forbede / but men shulde leve
> Wel more thing / than men han seen with eye   (1–11)

If we analyze the first 100 lines of the poem I think we can find twelve examples of the classical *cursus*:

planus

$(/ \times \times / \times)$	or found it writen	(8)
	sprad in the brightnesse	(64)
$(/ / / \times)$	and ful credence	(31)
	my devocion	(39)
	to yive credence	(97)

tardus

(/ / / × ×)	ye be diligent	(70)
	doon him reverence	(98)
	lady sovereyne	(94)

trochaicus

	weyes writen	(7)
	olde apprived stories	(21)
	sondry thynges	(23)
	in my labour	(71)

I should point out that when lifted out of their context and the significance of the virga ignored, the foregoing could be read differently. One thing that stands out clearly is that words, even French words, do not have to have their stresses shifted to fit the pattern. Another thing that becomes apparent is that in the verses of essentially English character in which it would be impossible to find the classic *cursus* there are subtle suggestions. Chaucer has achieved in the *Legend of Good Women* the verse to which he will give even greater subtlety in the *Canterbury Tales*. What Chaucer has achieved is the fusion of the basic speech rhythms, subtly modified by the *cursus* and its derivatives, and somewhat regularized by the French influence.

A second passage from the Prologue will further illustrate the quality of the verse:

I may not attones / speke in ryme
My besy gost / that trusteth alwey newe
To seen this flour / so yong / so fressh of hewe
Constreyned me / with so gledy desire
That in my herte / I feele yet the fire
That made me to ryse / er yt wer day
And was now / the firste morwe of May
With dredful hert / and glad devocion
for to ben / at the resureccion
Of this flour / whan yt shulde unclose
A gayne the sonne / that was as rede as rose
That in the brest was of the beste that day
That Agenours doghtre / ladde away
And doune on knes / anoon ryght I me sette
And as I koude / this fressh flour I grette
Knelyng alwey / til it unclosed was
Upon the smal softe / swote gras

That was with floures swote / embrouded al
Of swich swetnesse / and swich odour over al
That for to speke / of gome or herbe or tree
Comparison may noon / ymaked bee

(102–122)

Ten of the foregoing lines simply do not lend themselves to an iambic scansion. The eleven that can be forced into an iambic mold lose all subtlety when so forced; moreover the reader must ignore the significance of the virga to force them. The verse of the *Legend* shows greater freedom than that of previous poems, but it still has not attained to that of the *Troilus* or the *Canterbury Tales*.

An examination of some of the MSS. of *Troilus and Criseyde* reveals textual evidence in support of the hypothesis that Chaucer's prosody has a rhythmical rather than a metrical basis.

The practices of the scribes are various. The scribe of the Campsall MS. employs two marks—the virga and the low punctum. He used the virga with little regularity, but in every case the reading warrants a rise in the voice, or a level tone in American speech— ' Nor under cloud blak / so bright a sterre ' (I, 175).

This line merits detailed comment. In Campsall, there is no -e in *cloud* or *blak*; in Harleian 2280 and St. John's College, Cambridge, we have *cloude* and *blake*, both with final e; in Cambridge 427 and MS. 61 Corpus Christi College, Camb., we have *cloude* with a final -e and *blak* without it; in Harleian 1239, *cloud* with no final -e, but *blake* with one. Since I cannot go along with those scholars who think of the scribes either as careless or as having no understanding of the prosody of their day, only two of the four choices are possible without disturbing the essential rhythm. *Cloude blake* or *Cloud blake* would destroy the pattern because the virga calls for a rise or at least a level tone before it. We could have *cloude blak* or *cloud blak*. I am inclined to think that none of the final -e's was pronounced, particularly when we remember our earlier example of *hert sore*.

In Campsall IV, lines 841–847, the virga separates the words in series and indicates a single bar juncture (a lengthening of the phonemes before the break with a sustension of the pitch level across the break '—Roberts, 251).

Who-so me set, he set sorwe al at onys.
Peyne / torment / pleynt / wo / and distresse.
Out of my woful body / harm þer non is.

> As angwyssh / langour / cruel bitternesse.
> A-noy / smert / drede / fury / and ek sikenesse.
> I trowe I-wys from hevene teris reyne.
> For pite of myn aspre and cruwel peyne.

In MS. 61 Corpus Christi College and St. John's College, Cambridge, the scribes also placed a punctum at the end of every line, not only after direct statements but after questions. In American English, and quite possibly in Chaucerian English, the intonation falls at these junctures, whereas in modern British speech the intonation rises after a question:

> And þow my suster ful of discomfort,
> Quod Pandarus / what þenkestow to do.
> Whi ne hastow to þi-selven som resport.
> Whi / woltow þus þi-selve for-do
>
> (Campsall, IV, 848–851)

B. M. Harleian 2392, admittedly a good MS, will give us a better basis for testing our theory of Chaucer's prosody than we have so far had. In comparing the readings with those in Robinson we must remember that in his text ' grammatical errors have been corrected, especially incorrect -e's, as have also a few forms which appear not to be consistent with Chaucer's usage. Inflectional endings have occasionally been supplied when necessary for the meter or for clearness of meaning. But no attempt has been made at the regular restoration of unpronounced final -e's which are omitted rather more freely in the Corpus MS. than in the Ellesmere.' (*Chaucer's Complete Works*, p. 1024).

By whose authority did he feel justified in such emendations? By the authority of a dogmatic statement by Child, based on an unsupported assumption by Tyrwhitt, an assumption knocked into a cocked hat by G. B. Nott. I prefer to assume that only as the MSS. support us without serious emendation are we justified in any hypothesis.

As I have repeatedly mentioned, if we ignore the marks of punctuation which do literally enable us to hear the waves of speech, and if we ignore the testimony of the prose of the period, of poems written in known Latin meters and the possible influence of the cursus, a very large portion of Chaucer's verse can be made to fit into an iambic decasyllabic mold; that is, we can if we look upon every exception in the MSS. as the careless mistakes of the scribes.

But what of those hundreds of passages wherein the text itself does not permit such treatment? Let us confine ourselves to B. M. Harleian 2392.

I. 4   fro wo / to wele / and aftirward out of joie

Rhythmically the -*ward* of *aftirward* is satisfactory, but destroys an iambic reading. Robinson—*after*

I. 12   for wel sit it / the sothe al for to seyne

Usually the -*e* of *soethe* is presumed to be sounded. The presence of *al* would indicate that such was not the case. Robinson: the sothe for to seyne.

I. 24   remembreth yow / on old hevynesse

Old does not permit an iambic reading. If read with a rising tone in the arsis and a falling one in the thesis this is satisfactory. Robinson: *passed* for *old*

I. 71 ff.   So whan this Calkas / knew by calkelyng
            And eek by answere of this Appollo
            that Grekes shulde / such a pepill bryng
            thorough which that troye / shold be fordo
            he cast anon / out of the town to go
            ffor wiste he be sort that troye shold
            destroied be / ye wolde he so nold

To fit the foregoing into the metrical mold demands inconsistency in pronunciation.

I. 122   ye shul have / and your body men shul save

It is possible, by ignoring the position of the virga and by pronouncing final -*e*'s usually silent to scan the other six lines of this stanza as iambic. But the presence of the foregoing line—unscannable by any metrical pattern—would indicate that the scribe had not heard the other lines as iambic.

Let us make a few comparisons of the text of Harleian 2392 and Robinson's text.

I. 657   Nay never yit / quod ywis troylis
         (Robinson) ' Nay nevere yet, ywys,' quod Troilus

I. 694   The wise eek seith / wo hym that is alone
              ' The wise seith, " wo hym that is allone ".'

I. 688   mystrusten al / or ellis al leve
                             Mistrusten alle, or elles alle leve

I. 723   but longe he lay stille / as he ded were
                             But longe he lay as stylle as he ded were

I. 729   And saide / awak fool / wonderli sharp
                             And cryde 'Awak! ' ful wonderlich and sharpe

I. 744   that toucheth love / that ought ben secre
                             that toucheth love that oughte ben secree

II. 95   to herken of your book / that ye preisen thus
                             To herken of youre book ye preysen thus

II. 164   for treuly / I hold gret deynte
                             For trewelich I holde it gret deynte,

      (The pointing of Harleian gives a better reading than that of Robinson)

II. 262   What sholde I peynt it / or drawe on lengthe
                             What sholde I peynte or drawen it on lengthe

An interesting example that throws light on the pronunciation and therefore on the rhythm occurs in Book III.

III. 8–10   In hevene / in helle / in erthe / in salt se
                             is felt thi miht / if that I myght discerne
                             as man / bird / beste / fissh / herbe / and grene tre

I think ' in salt se ' and ' and grene tre ' would each be read as × / /.

III. 98   was thries / mercy √[1] mercy / my diere herte
Rob.   Was, twyes, ' Mercy, mercy swete herte! '

III. 125, 126   to telle the fin / of his hol entent
                             yet wiste I never weel / what he ment
Rob.   To telle me the fyn of his entente.
                             Yet wist I nevere wel what that he mente.

III. 326   but weel wot I / in wismen / that vice
R.   For wel woot I, in wise folk that vice

III. 404   departe it so / for wide wher it is wist
R.   Departe it so; for wyde wher is wist

III. 802, 3   allas / I wende who that talis tolde
                             my deere herte / wolde not holde
                             so lihtli me fals /

[1] The mark in the MS. more nearly resembles that in the Ellesmere. See note p. 27

R.   ' allas! I wende, whoso tales tolde,
             My deere herte wolde me nought holde
             So lightly fals!'

V. 1795ff.   so pray I to god / that non myswrite the
             ne the mys / metre / for defaute of tonge
             and red / where so thou be / or ellis songe
             that thou be understonde / god I beseche
             but yit to purpos / of my rathere speche.

The foregoing illustrations are merely a few of those that appear on every page. I firmly believe that Harleian 2392 gives us a clearer indication of contemporary pronunciation than do those MSS. written by scribes more conservative in their spelling.

But what support do we get from other MSS. of the *Troilus*? Harleian 2280 (H1) uses no mark of punctuation in the early folios. The virga first appears after stanza 77. (Incidentally, in stanza one, *joye* is one word, *fro ye* is clearly two; in Harleian 2392 (H4) 1. 4 ends in *ioie*, 1. 5 in *fro the* which indicates that neither scribe thought of the lines as rhyming.) Many scholars, not understanding that the virga, often very faint indeed, was a guide to the person reading the MS. aloud, have been puzzled by the fact that the marks do not always occur at the same places in every MS. If as early investigators thought, this mark indicated the caesura, then clearly the marks should occur at the same place in every MS.; but since they are essentially intonational marks, they would indicate the different readings. My experience has been that in every case, if these marks are heeded, the reading is good. The marks in some MSS. indicate a very subtle reading.

Who was responsible for these marks? The scribe or the poet? I am inclined to believe that the poet himself was responsible for most of them. It is possible that when they differ from MS. to MS. we have evidence of the author's revisions. On the other hand, if some one was dictating the MSS. to a group of scribes, then quite possibly the marks were those of the scribe determined by the manner in which the poem was dictated. But of one thing we can be certain. Whoever was responsible for them possessed a good ear. The following from Harleian 2392 reveals a different punctuation from Harleian 2280, as well as some changes in the text. These changes would indicate that the iambic pentameter system of prosody was not in the scribe's mind.

E

Madame / quod pandare / god you see
With alle your bookes / and your companye
ey uncle / welcome y wis quod she
and up she ros / and bi the hond in hie
she took hym faste / and seide these nyhtis thre
to good mut it turne / of you I mette
and with that word / she doun on bench hir sette

Ye nece / ye shul fare moche the bette
yf god wole / al this yeer / quod pandarus
but I am sory / that I have you lette
to herken of your book / that ye preisen thus
for godis loue / what it seith / tell us
is it of loue / som good ye me lere
Uncle quod she / your maistresse is not heere
(Harleian 2392, II, 85–98)

Quod pandarus / madame god ʒow see
Wt al ʒoure fair book / and alle þe compaignye
Ey uncle myn / welcome ywys quod she
And up she roos / and by þe hond in hye
She took hym fast / and seyd this nyght thrye
To goode mote it torne / of ʒow I mette
and wt þat worde she doun on bench hym sette.

Ye nece / ʒe shal faren wel þe bette
If god wole / alle þis ʒere quod Pandarus
But I am sory þat I have ʒow lette
To herknen of ʒoure book ʒe preisen þus
ffor goddes loue / what syth it tel it us
Is it of loue / o som goode ʒe me leere
uncle quod she / ʒour maistresse is not heere
(II, 85–98)

Harley 3943 (H2) uses no marks of punctuation. Root does not record all the variations of the text, and there are fewer final unaccented *e*'s in this text: *hall-all-fall*; *awow-rescow*. Additional 12044, rhyming words with or without final *-e* peyne-pleyne-seyn—, differs slightly from both Harleian 2392 and Harleian 2280, but all three readings have a delightful colloquial movement. Additional 12044 sometimes goes for pages with no marks of punctuation. Occasionally the scribe makes an error in copying. In III, 1153, for example, instead of writing ' She bad hym to telle hir bisily ' the scribe's eye, seeing the previous line 'And ek the sygne þat he took it by,' copied it as ' She bad him that he took it by,' which, of course, makes no sense and is an obvious mistake.

It would be a simple matter to multiply the instances of lines in the various MSS. that do not scan according to a metrical system of prosody. Just before the lovely aubade in Book III, for example, Harleian 2392, 1. 1397 reads ' and eek rehersyn / how / whane / and wheere.' The marks play an important part, too, in assisting the reader to capture the swelling emotion of the aubade, so anticipatory of that in *Romeo and Juliet*. There are enough echoes of *Troilus and Criseyde* in Shakespeare's *Merchant of Venice*, *Midsummer Night's Dream* and *Romeo and Juliet* to warrant our thinking that Shakespeare had been reading carefully the edition of the *Troilus* published just before the period of these plays.

> O blak nyht / as folk in bokis reede
> that shapen art bi god / this word to hide
> that certeyn tymes / with the blak weede
> that undir that / men myhte in reste a bide
> Weel ouhte bestus pleyne / and folk the chide
> that there as day / with labour wolde us breste
> that thou thus fleest / and deynest us not to reste
>
> Thou dost allas / so shortly thin office
> thou rakil nyht / ther god maker of kynde
> for thou so downward / hastest of malice
> thi cours / and to our emyspherie bynde
> that nevermo / undir the grounde thou wynde
> for though thi rakil / þeeng out of troie
> have I forgon thus hastily / my joie
>
> This troilus / that bi tho wordes felte
> as thouhte him tho / for pitous distresse
> the blody teris / from his herte melte
> as he that nevere yit / such hevynesse
> assaied had / out of so gret gladnesse
> gan therwithal / cressaide his lady deere
> in armys streyne / and seide in this maneere

O cruel day / accusere of the joie
that love and nyht / han stole and faste y wreien
a cursed be thi comyng / into troie
for every bor / hath of thi briht yen
envious day / what lust the so tespien
what hast thou lost / what sechist thou in this place
there god this liht / se quenche for his grace

Allas / what han these loveres the agilt
Dispitous day / thyn be the peyne of hell
for a many lovere / host thou slayn and wilt
thi pouryng / wil we non heere / let us duell
What profrest thou / liht heere for to sell
go sell it them / that smale selis grave
We wil the not / us nedith no day to have   (1429–1463)

From the number of lines in the foregoing passage that do not
scan as iambic decasyllables, however one thinks of final unaccented
-e, it is impossible to believe that the scribe conceived of the prosody
as other than rhythmic.

The nature of the rime royal stanza with its rigid rhyme pattern,
a-b-a-b-b-c-c, does not lend itself to the same type of rhythmical
subtlety that is possible with the couplet, just as the couplet sets
limitations to the rhythmical liberties enjoyed by a writer of blank
verse. This is not to deny subtlety of rhythmical effect to any form
whatever when used by a master. How rigid a limitation the exigencies of rhyme laid on poets who could not find freedom within such
a set pattern is evident in the work of Hoccleve, Lydgate and others.
The rime royal stanza can be a crutch for the uninspired poet and
somewhat of a shackle to an inspired one. When Chaucer turned
to the *Canterbury Tales* after his efforts in verses of cadence, in rime
royal, in poems in which he was influenced by the Italian canzone,
and other forms, he had achieved a flexibility that reveals itself fully
in the *Canterbury Tales*, where we shall find that all the various
rhythms attempted by him are beautifully fused into a new and
unique voice.

CHAPTER III

THE CANTERBURY TALES

The Ellesmere MS. of the *Canterbury Tales*, as I have said, makes extensive use of three marks of punctuation: the virga (/) within the line, the √ at the end of a line where the voice is to be suspended because the meaning is not completed until the following verse, and the √[1] to indicate a question. This √ was used in Gower's *Confessio Amantis*, Bodl. Fairfax 3, but there it did not indicate a definite question. Interestingly enough, the √ occurs chiefly in the E-group. The following passages are typical:

E. 106–111   ffor certes lord / so wel us liketh yow
                And al youre werk / and ever han don / that we√
                Ne koude nat us self devysen how √
                We myghte lyven / in moore felicitee
                Save o thyng lord / if youre wille be
                That . . .

E. 157–161   Bountee comth al of god / nat of the streen
                Of which / they been engendred and ybore
                I truste in goddes bontee / and therefore √
                My mariage / and myn estaat and reste
                I hym bitake / be may doon as hym leste

E. 169, 170   And forthermoore / this shall ye swere / that ye √
                Agayn my choys / shul neither grucche ne stryve

E. 319–321   But oonly thus / lord quod he / my willynge √
                Is as ye wole / ne ageyns / youre likynge √
                I wol no thing . . .

E. 359, 360   She seyde lord / undigne and unworthy √
                Am I / to thilke honour / that ye me beede

E. 373–375   And for that no thyng / of hir olde geere
                She sholde brynge in to his hous he bad √
                That women / sholde dispoillen hyr right theere

E. 1258, 9   Preyinge oure lord / to graunten him that he √
                Mighte ones knowe / of thilke blisful lyf . . .

[1] Although similar to but less angular, it is *not* a *punctus elevatus*.

E. 1386–8   No man hateth his flessh / but in his lyf √
              He fostreth it / and therfore bidde I thee
              Cherisse thy wyf /
F. 2, 3   . . . for certes ye √
              Konnen ther on as muche as any man

The scribe does not use the question mark √ nearly so often as does a modern editor, and only rarely does he use it where the modern editor would omit it. These instances, however, throw light on the contemporary method of reading.

A. 1123–25   This Palamon / whan he tho wordes herde
              Dispitously / he looked and answerde
              Wheither seistow this / in ernest or in pley √
A. 3487–90   And atte laste this hende Nicholas
              Gan for to sike soore / and seyde allas
              Shal al this world / be lost eftsoones now√
              This carpenter answerde / What seystow√
A. 3781–83   Thou sholdest have as I am trewe smyth
              Ey cristes foo / what wol ye do ther with√
A. 3790–93   This Alison answerde / who is ther √
              That knokketh so / I warante it a theef
              Why nay quod he / god woot my sweete leef
              I am thyn Absolon / my deerelyng

The position of this mark sometimes requires a different intonation than modern punctuation permits.

B. 498–501   Where myghte this womman / mete and drynke have√
              Thre yeer and moore / how lasteth hyr vittaille√
              Who fedde the Egiptien Marie in the cave√
              Or in desert √ ne wight but crist sanz faille

Robinson's punctuation connects ' thre yeer and moore ' with ' mete and drynke ' rather than with ' vitaille '. The same is true of his pointing of B. 971–973. The punctuation of the MS. is more subtle.

              No thyng knew he / what she was ne why√
              She was in swich array / ne she nyl seye
              Of hir estaat / thogh she sholde deye
Robinson.   Nothyng ne knew he what she was, ne why
              She was in swich array, ne she nyl seye
              Of hire estaat, although she sholde deye

It is not a question of why she was in such array, but rather that because she was in such array that she would not confess her identity. A strict attention to the intonation dictated by the two marks of punctuation captures the urgent pleading quality that Robinson's punctuation fails to do in the following from the Wife of Bath's Tale:

D. 1088–1097 ffareth every knyght / thus with his wyf / as ye√
Is this the lawe / of kyng Arthures hous√
Is every knyght of his so dangerous √
I am youre owene love and youre wyf
I am she / which that saved hath youre lyf
And certes / yet ne did I yowe never unright
Why fare ye thus with me this firste nyght√
Ye faren lyk a man / had lost his wit
What is my gilt √ for goddes love tel it
And it shal ben amended if I may

The scribe also uses the √ to warn that anap positive follows the pronoun as for example, in E. 2021–2024 to indicate that *This noble Januaire* stands in apposition to the preceding *he*.

Some clerkes holden that felicitee
Stant in delit / and therfore certeyn he√
This noble Januarie / with al his myght
In honest wyse /

Or he may make a mistake, as when he uses a √ for a √ — Why speke ye thus √ which is obviously a question.

The use of the virga in the Ellesmere helps one to capture much of Chaucer's subtlety that disappears if one reads the lines as iambic pentameter. It is true that if one disregards the position of the virga hundreds of lines in the *Prologue* alone can be forced into the iambic pentameter mold. If, however, the reader observes the intonational pattern at these junctures—the single-barred juncture which I have already mentioned—the pattern changes. But what of those lines that simply cannot be so forced? Here is a sampling:

And wonderly delyvere / and of greet strengthe   (84)
And by his syde / a swerd / and a bokeler   (112)
Hir gretteste ooth / was but by Seint loy   (120)
In curteisie / was set ful muchel hir list
Hir over lippe / wyped she so clene

That in hir coppe / ther was no ferthyng sene
Of grece / Whan she dronken had hir draughte
fful semely / aftir hir mete she raughte   132-136

(The virga after *lippe* and *grece* would prevent the final -*e* from being sounded, even for those who think it should be, and the presence in the MSS. of marks indicating a carry over of the sense from one line to another would prevent the pronunciation of final -*e* in *sene* and *draughte*.)

As seyde hym self / moore than a curat   (219)
His nekke / whit was / as the flour delys   (238)
And everich hostiler / and Tappestere   (241)
In lovedayes / ther koude he muchel help   (258)
In motlee / and hye on horse he sat   (271)
Ther wiste no wight / that he was in dette   (280)
That un to logyk / hadde longe ygo   (286)
ffor hym was levere / have at his beddes heed   (293)
But al be / that he was a philosophre
Yet hadde he but litel gold in cofre   (297, 8)
That often hadde been at the parvys   (310)
Ther koude no wight / pynchen at his writing   (326)
Wel loved he by the morwe a sop in wyn
To lyven in delit / was evere his wone   (334, 5)
Was verray felicitee parfit   (338)
And many a breem / and many a luce in stuwe
 4 3 3 3   2 2 2 3   3
Wo was his cook but if his sauce were
 3 2   2 3   2 3 2 2 2 1
Poynaunt and sharp / and redy for his gere   (350-352)

(The pronunciation of *sauce* has puzzled me. Was the final -*e* sounded in such locutions as *sauce depe*? It may possibly have been, but the rhythm of the foregoing lines demands that in this case the *e* of *sauce* should not be sounded. I have indicated the intonational pitch pattern as I hear the lines. The un-English quality of the expression, noun plus adjective, is responsible for the tendency to pronounce final -e.)
 2 3 2 3 3   3 3 3 2 1
In al the parisshe / wif ne was ther noon   (449)

Although the scribe makes abundant use of the virga in the Prologue, he does not use it as fully as he does in many of the tales. The scribe of the Hengwrt makes a much greater use of it than does he of the Ellesmere. A careful collation of the two MSS. reveals, too, that the pointing in the Hengwrt is far more subtle than that of the Ellesmere. A collation with Additional 5140 further reveals that where the Ellesmere and the Hengwrt differ, Additional 5140 agrees first with one and then with the other.

What is true of the *Prologue* is also true of the *Tales*. The following isolated lines from the Miller's Prologue in the Ellesmere, amended by Robinson, are clearly not iambic decasyllabic. The absence of the virga in the first line suggests a more rapid movement:

> Oure host saugh that he was dronke of ale
> And seyde / abyd Robyn my leeve brother
> Som bettre man / shal telle us first another
>
> (A. 3128–30)

Line 3128 scans as follows: $\times$ / / $\times$ $\times$ $\times$ / $\times$ $\times$

> / $\times$ $\times$ / $\times$ / $\times$ $\times$ $\times$
> Wyte it / the ale of Southwerk I preye   (A. 3140)

> $\times$ / $\times$ $\times$ / $\times$ $\times$ / $\times$ $\times$
> Avyseth yow putteth me out of blame   (A. 3185)

The foregoing are mere random samplings, but if we find three lines within so short a space that even by the most arbitrary rules of pronunciation do not scan with any marked regularity, and the intervening lines only on the supposition that the rules of pronunciation current for prose do not apply to poetry, a reader is justified in being skeptical. Incidentally the three lines all end in the *cursus tardus*, an example of cadence. In the *Tale* itself it is readily apparent that a very sophisticated person is speaking—no drunken miller. Except for line 3226, the pointing of the Ellesmere and Hengwrt is the same. In the Ellesmere the virga falls after *lik*, in the Hengwrt, after *self*. The pause after *self* suggests slyness on the part of the narrator, aiming for a surprise effect, as in 3226:

> Of XVIII yeer / she was of age
> Jalous he was / and heeld hire narwe in cage
> ffor she was wilde and yong / and he was old
> And demed hym self / been lyk a cokewold
> He knew nat Caton / for his wit was rude
> That bad / man sholde wedde his similitude
> Men sholde wedden / after hir estaat

ffor youthe and elde / is often at debaat
But sith þt he / was fallen in the snare
he moste endure / as oother folk his care
(Hengwrt: A. 3223-3332)

The pointing of the Hengwrt and the Ellesmere in the detailed
description of the young wife is far more subtle than that found in
any modern text. Robinson's punctuation may be grammatically
correct, but it suggests none of the sly humour of the original. It is
obvious that he was not hearing what the person who had punctuated the MS. wished him to near.

Or when we turn to the opening of the Reve's Tale, as unsubtle
an opening as one could imagine, it is obvious that Chaucer is
satirizing the Reve who has read too many metrical romances. Of
the first four lines three have the dreadful monotony of *Sir Thopas*
and one doesn't scan:

At Trompyngton / nat fer fro Cantebrygge
Ther gooth a brook / and over that a brygge
Up on the which brook / ther stant a melle
And this is verray sooth / þt I yow telle
(Hengwrt: A. 3921-3924)

Later in the story the dialogue loosens somewhat but none of the
subtle rhythm of the *Miller's Tale* is present. The most sparing use
of the virga occurs in those tales ascribed to women narrators. The
Wife of Bath as we have noticed tells her tale with an almost breath-
less garrulity.

The subtlest use, as well as the most extensive use of the virga, is
found in *The Pardoner's Tale*. The pardoner's speech, too, makes
frequent use of the *curses*:

tardus (/ / / × ×)

to devocion	(346)
heeleth jalousie	(366)
se my bisynesse	(399)
of swich cursednesse	(400)
in conclusion	(454)
John, ful giltelees	(491)
good word doutelees	(492)
ful of cursednesse	(498)

tardus (/ × × / × ×)

	yvel entencioun	(408)
	develes officeres	(480)
planus		
	body to warente	(338)
	putte in this mitayn	(373)
	haunteden folye	(464)
trochaicus		
	on my patente	(337)
	cardynales	(342)

(The *trochaicus* occurs so frequently that one tends to forget that it is a form of *cursus*.)

The foregoing is only a sampling from a small portion of the story. Examples of verses of cadence occur more frequently in the tales told by persons in holy orders, and naturally so since their ears were constantly bombarded with a prose style making extensive use of the *cursus*.

In the following passage from the *Pardoner's Tale*, notice the tenseness of the lines up to 389, and then the relaxation immediately following. The pardoner is offering the *sholder-boon* that will perform miracles:

> And sire / also / it heeleth jalousie
> ffor though a man / be falle in jalous rage
> Lat maken with this water his potage
> And never shal he more / his wyf mystriste
> Though he the soothe / of hir defaute wiste   370
> Al had she / taken preestes / two or thre
> Heere is a miteyn eek / that ye may se
> He þat his hand wol putte in this mitayn
> He shal have / multipliyng / of his grayn
> Whan he hath sowen / be it whete or otes   375
> So þat he offre / pens / or elles grotes
> Goode men and women / o thyng warne I yow
> If any wight / be in this chirche now
> That hath donne synne horrible þat he√
> Dar not for shame / of it yshryven be   380
> Or any woman / be she yong or old
> That hath ymaked / hir housbonde cokewold
> Swich folk / shal have no power ne no grace

> To offren / to my relikes in this place
> And who so fyndeth hym / out of swich fame   385
> They wol come up / and offre on goddes name
> And I assoille hem / by the auctoritee
> Which that by bulle / ygraunted was to me
> By this gaude / have I wonne / yeer by yeer
> An hundred mark / sith I was pardoner
> I stonde lyk a clerk / . . .
>   (Ellesmere : C366–391)

By carefully observing the significance of the single bar juncture (a slight pause at the virga with a level pitch intonation), lines 369, 370, 371, and 375 convey an ironic implication not apparent with traditional punctuation. The Pardoner's Tale of the three rioters has a different tone from the foregoing, the tone of a master story-teller. The opening lines afford matter for speculation.

> Thise riotours thre / of whiche I telle
> Longe erst / er prime rong of any belle
> Were set hem / in a taverne to drynke
> And as they sat / they herde a belle clynke
> Biforn a cors / was caried / to his grave
> That oon of hem / gan callen to his knave
> Go bet quod he and axe redily
> What cors is this / þat passeth heer forby
> And looke / þat thou reporte his name weel
>   (Ellesmere: C661–669)

The differences in pointing of the Hengwrt in the two foregoing passages are slight but significant. The scribe places a virga after *water* (368), *putte* (373), *horrible* (379), *power* (383), *relikes* (384), instead of after *offren* (386). The reading of line 376 is more deliberate and more emphatic: 'So þt / he / offre pens / or ellis grotes.' Line 385 has *blame* instead of *fame*.

Line 665 omits the / after *caryed*, places one after *he* (667).

The spelling of *riotours* (both in Ellesmere and Hengwrt), emended by Robinson to *riotoures*, does not permit of an iambic scansion. Was the *e* of *prime* sounded? Of 24 instances of *prime* listed in the *Concordance*, 20 unquestionably have the *e* silent. Besides the foregoing example where there might be some question, we have the following from the *Squiers' Tale* and 2 from *Troilus and Criseyde*. The first, tells us nothing—They slepen / til that it was pryme large

(F 360). Those from *Troilus* do. The pitch intonation indicated by

the virga precludes the pronunciation of final *e*: And eek so lik a

soth / at prime face (*T & C* 3. 919); fful redy was at prime / Diomede
(T & C 5. 15).

Or was the *e* of *belle* sounded in 1. 564? Again having recourse
to the *Concordance* we find *belle* listed 16 times. Only three are in
a position where the iambic pattern demands the sounding of the *e*.
The other two are from *Troilus*. In Harleian 2392, neither example
spells *bell* with a final -*e*, and so could not have sounded one: ' for
this miracle / I heer ech bell sowne ' (3. 189); ' thoruhout the world
/ my bell shal be ronge ' (6. 1062). The chances are, therefore, that
the final *e* of *belle* was not sounded.

The third instance in this passage is *name* in 1. 669. Of some 160
entries from poetry in the *Concordance*, only 13 instances require
the final *e* to satisfy the iambic pattern. Robinson's text agrees more
with that of Harleian 2392, in which the final *e* was definitely not
sounded: ffor weel thou wost / the name as yit of hire (*T. C.* 3.
267). If the reader heeds the intonational marks, however, it is clear
that Chaucer did not think of these lines as iambic. A Kn 1586, for
example, in the Ellesmere is as follows: 'And falsly / chaunged hast /
thy name thus '; and every line which demands the final *e* in *name* for
the iambic pattern does not sound it in the rhythmical pattern.

Two words, the pronunciation of which disturbed me, were
pale and *face*. It struck me that *palë face* and *facë pale* sounded pleasanter than when the final *e* of the first word was not sounded. But
the evidence supports the non-pronuncation of final *e* in each case.
Take the case of *pale*. The Concordance lists 61 instances of it in
the poetry. Of these instances 52 do not permit final *e* in the iambic
pattern; 9 call for it. In the Ellesmere, A Kn 1998 reads ' The
pykepurs / and the pale drede.' Robinson uses the reading from the
Hengwrt: ' The pykepurs, and eek the pale Drede.' The omission of
eek in the Ellesmere is significant. The second instance, A Kn 2443,
' Til that the pale / Saturnus the colde,' having the virga after *pale*
precludes the possibility of sounding the final -*e*. The third instance
is perhaps more subjective. In the Ellesmere, B. ML. 645, occurs as
follows:

Have ye not seyn / somtyme a pale face

The position of the virga controls the intonation pattern. The fourth instance (B. ML. 822) is a matter for the reader; although read in context, I think an unsounded final *e* heightens the solemnity:

<pre>
2   3 3   3   2 2 2 3   2
And Custance / With a deedly pale face
2   3   3   3 2   2   2   2   1
The ferthe day / toward hir ship she wente
</pre>

The fifth instance (E. Cl. 340) supports the case for not sounding the *e*:

<pre>
2   3   3   3 2   2   3   2   1
Ffor which she looked / with ful pale face
</pre>

I do not think it necessary to examine BD. 497, TC. 5. 536, RR. 7255 or RR. 7394. Since Child thought, as I have several times mentioned, that final *e* was just beginning to go out in Chaucer's day, there is some excuse for his thinking that in most words it could or could not be pronounced depending on the exigencies of the rhythm. There is no excuse for modern scholars clinging to this outmoded idea. If *e* had ceased being sounded in the prose we can be certain that the poets were not sounding it in their poetry. A poet can always fit the current pronunciation of a word into his prosodic pattern; not only can, but must. Although the pronunciation of *pale face* or *face pale* cannot be absolutely determined, I think the basic difficulty is that in the locution *face pale* is essentially un-English, and being so the reader attempts to compensate for the un-English quality by sounding the final -*e* of *face*. In other words, he attempts to transform a locution that offers no problem in French intonation with both final *e*'s mute to the wavelike intonation of English.

Since the purpose of this study is not an aesthetic appreciation of Chaucer's art but an attempt to establish on sound evidence the nature of Chaucer's prosody, it is important that we compare the different MSS. The fact that the virga does not always appear at the same places in the various MSS. of the same work has given rise to the question as to who is responsible for the differences, the poet or the scribe. Since the marks often indicate that one reading is more subtle than another it is tempting to think that the more subtle reading is a revision of the author's earlier reading. We shall probably never know. But at least a careful sampling of the differences will heighten our respect for the poets of the 14C.

Scholars have been unduly disturbed by this fact. The scholar familiar with the successive drafts of modern poets writing in a rhythmical tradition would find nothing peculiar in it. In that remarkable collection of MSS. of modern poets in the University of Buffalo libary, for example, in the papers of William Carlos Williams there are twelve versions of one short poem. The changes that occur in the successive versions are subtle changes reflecting the poet's search for the right intonation. A word at the end of the line might be moved to the position of first word in the following line. The effect is at first unnoticeable. The same is true of the position of the virga in the Chaucerian MSS. In general, I find greater rhythmical subtlety in the Hengwrt than in the Ellesmere. Do the changes represent Chaucer's own modifications? It is tempting to think so. But a wish is not sufficient grounds for a hypothesis, although several 19C scholars acted as if it were. But let us examine some of these differences in the description of the Squyer. If the reader treats the virga as indicating the single-bar juncture of the modern linguists the difference in the opening couplet is a subtle one.

Ellesmere.

Squier	With hym ther was his sone a yong squier	
	A louyere / and a lusty bacheler	
	Wt lokkes crulle / as they were leyd in presse	
	Of twenty yeer of age / he was I gesse	
	Of his stature / he was of evene lengthe	
	And wonderly delyuere / and of greet strengthe	
	And he hadde been somtyme in chyvachie	85
	In fflaundres / in Artoys and Pycardie	
	And born hym weel / as of so litel space	
	In hope / to stonden in his lady grace	
	Embrouded was he / as it were a meede	
	Al ful of fresshe floures / whyte and rede	90
	Syngynge he was / or floytynge al the day	
	He was as fressh / as is the monthe of may	
	Short was his gowne / wt sleues longe and wyde	
	Wel koude he sitte on hors and faire ryde	
	He koude songes make / and wel endite	95
	Juste Â eek daunce / and weel purtreye Â write	
	So hoote he louede / that by nyghtertale	
	He slepte namoore than dooth a nyghtyngale	
	Curteis he was / lowely / and seruysable	
	And carf / biforn his fader at the table	100

Hengwrt.

Squyer   With hym / ther was his sone a yong Squyer
         A louere and a lusty bachiler
         With lokkes crulle / as they were leyd in p'sse
         Of : xx . yeer he was of age I gesse
         Of his stature / he was of evene lengthe
         And wonderly delyuere / and of greet strengthe
         And he hadde been somtyme in chi [vachi]e   85
         In fflaundres / in Artoys / and . Picardye
         And born hym wel / as in so litel space
         In hope / to stonden / in his lady grace
         Embrouded was he / as it weere a meede
         Al ful of fresshe floures / white and rede   90
         Synginge he was / or floytynge al the day
         He was as fressh / as is the monthe of may
         Short was his gowne / with sleues / longe â wyde
         Wel koude he sitte on hors / and faire ryde
         he koude songes wel make / and endite   95
         Juste and eek daunce / and wel purtreye and wryte
         So hoote he loved that by nyghtertale
         He slepte namoore / than dooth a nyghtyngale
         Curteys he was . lowely / and seruysable
         And carf biforn his fader / at the table   100

                              (*Prol.* 11. 79–100.)

The pointing of Hengwrt gives a subtler and wittier reading than
does Ellesmere.

The virga after *hym* (79), for example, intensifies the conversational quality. There is no reason to separate the elements in 1. 80.
The difference in word order in l. 82 makes the virga unnecessary.
By placing a virga after *Artoys* and a low punctum after *and* in l. 86,
the poet varies the tempo of the verse. One can hear the reader
hasten to add 'And born hym wel ' after the preceding pauses. The
virga after *stonden* as well as after *hope* gives just such a subtle reading
as a modern poet writing rhythmically achieves when he places a
word at the end of a line rather than at the beginning of the following
one. The slight pause after *stonden* heightens the reader's curiosity;
the Ellesmere pause after *hope* does little. Incidentally, *fresshe* in line
90 occurs in Add. 5140 without the final *-e*. The same subtlety occurs
in line 93 with the virga after *sleves* as well as after *gowne*. Was the

Squier being strictly Ivy League in his dress (when Ivy League was high style) or was he being ultra conservative? The pause after *sleves* raises the question. But no, he was dressed in the high style ridiculed by Hoccleve. The virga after *hors* in l. 94 conveys a sense of admiration, rather than the matter-of-fact tone of Ellesmere. The absence of a pause in the description of the squire loving (97) captures his own impetuosity. The Virga after *fader* better conveys the sense than does Ellesmere.

Risking the danger of overstressing the obvious let us examine three versions of the *General Prologue*, primarily from the point of view of the pointing but also from the point of view of the way in which textual variations in Additional 5140 throw light on the nature of the prosody.

Line 6 *Inspired hath in every holt | and heeth*
The virga follows *hath* in Ellesmere and Additional 5140. Additional 5140, however, omits the *in*. This is obviously an error on the part of the scribe, but it arises from the pause that the virga would indicate. Hengwrt puts a slight pause after *holt*, none after *hath*.

Line 7 *The tendre croppes | and the yonge sonne*
Add. 5140, like Hengwrt, has a virga after *croppes*, Ellesmere none. Add. 5140 spells *yong* without the *-e*. The scansion would be
/ × / /
and the yong sonne.

Line 8. Neither the Hengwrt, Ellesmere, or Add. 5140 have *halve*. The spelling is *half*. Add. 5140 also omits *his*. It cannot be scanned as iambic, but it does scan to capture the rhythms of speech.
/ × × / \ / / × /
Hath in the ram / his half cours yronne

Line 14 *To ferne halwes | kouthe in sondry landes*
Ellesmere omits the virga after *halwes*. Add. 5140 omits the final *-e* in *fern*. Rhythmically the music is subtle; Add. 5140 is impossible from the point of view of the iambic pattern.
× / / \ / × / × / ×
To fern halwes / kouthe in sondry landes
The second half of the line is obviously a *cursus trochaicus*.

Line 16 *Of Engelond | to Caunterbury they wende*
The Three MSS. agree on the virga after *Engelond*. Add. 5140 omits the medial *-e* and spells it *Englond*.

F

\ / /   \ / × / × ×   /

Of Englond / to Caunterbury they wende

The end of the line is an English *cursus planus*.

Line 18   *That hem hath holpen | whan that they weere seeke*

Add. 5140 omits the *that: whan they weere seeke*. The omission kills any iambic pattern: it only lays a slight additional stress on *whan* in the rhythmical scansion.

\ / ×   / \   \   / ×   /

That hem hath holpen / whan they weere seeke

The omission could easily be passed over, but it would have been glaring in an iambic pattern.

Line 20   *Redy to wenden | on my pilgrymage*

Neither Ellesmere nor Add. 5140 place a virga after wenden.

/ × ×   /   / × / × /

Add. 5140 alters the line: Redy to wende in my pilgrymage

Line 30   *And shortly | whan the sonne was to reste*

Ellesmere omits the virga. Add. 5140 reads: *And shortly whanne the son was gon to reste*. This would indicate that the final *e* in *sonne* was not sounded.

Line 39   *Of eech of hem | so as it seemed me.*

This can be scanned iambically in Hengwrt and Ellesmere, but not in Add. 5140, which omits the *so*. I prefer it, however, scanned rhythmically.

\ / × /   \ / \ / ×   \

Of eech of hem / so as it semed me.

The omission of the *so* makes little difference.

Line 49   *And ther to hadde he ryden | no man ferre*

The virga after *ryden* demands that each word of *no man ferre* be stressed. Add. 5140 reads: *And ther had ryden | no man so ferre*. This reading is probably not so good as Hengwrt and Ellesmere, but it communicates a sense of admiration.

Line 52   *fful ofte tyme | he hadde the bord bigonne*

Add. 5140 omits *tyme* and omits the final *e* in *oft*: fful oft he hadde / the boord begonne.

One could go on. There are literally hundreds of instances in the *General Prologue* of Add. 5140 that differ from the readings of Hengwrt and Ellesmere that would preclude its being read as iambic decasyllabic lines. There are also innumerable variations between the Hengwrt and the Ellesmere. In order for a modern editor to achieve a text that reads as iambic decasyllabic he has had to resort to a pastiche. Even Manly's text does not give the true picture.

The Hengwrt text of the *Pardoner's Prologue and Tale* in the Appendix will better enable the independent scholar to study an extensive piece of evidence. More interesting for our immediate purpose, however, is the use of the virga for the achievement of greater subtlety. Let us examine some individual lines. Lines 19ff. of Hengwrt have a more conversational tone than is possible in the Ellesmere or Additional 5140. The virga after *seson, Tabard, wenden, Caunterbury* and *come* indicate a non-iambic rhythm:

> Bifel *þt* in that seson / on a day
> [In] Southwerk at the Tabard / as I lay
> Redy to wenden / on my pilgrymage
> To Caunterbury / with ful devout corage
> At nyght was come / in to that hostelrye . . .

Lines 37–39 furnish another example, of which there are many on every folio page:

Hengwrt: Me thynketh it / accordant to resoun
          To telle yow / al the condicioun
          Of eech of hem / so as it seemed me
Add. 5140: Me thynkyth / it accordith on to reasoun
          To telle yow / of alle here condicioun
          Of eche of hem / as it semed me
Ellesmere: Me thynketh it acordaunt to resoun
          To telle yow al the condicioun
          Of ech of hem / so as it semed me

Hengwrt indicates the speech rhythms more clearly and accurately than the others. English speech, unlike that of French, has a wave-like quality, a quality visible in the description of the Knight.

The Hengwrt also introduces an element of suspense. In line 69: *And of his poort / as meke / as is a mayde.* Ellesmere and Add. 5140 have no virga after *meke.* The slight pause that the virga indicates gives a sly twist to what follows. A similar effect occurs in lines 152, 153:

Hengwrt: Hir nose tretes / hir eyen / greye as glas
          Hir mouth ful smal / and there to / softe and reed

Ellesmere and Add. 5140 have no virga after *eyen* or *ther to.* Add. 5140 has *streght* instead of *tretes.* Or in line 226:

Hengwrt: Is signe / that a man / is wel yshryve

Add. 5140 has no virga in the line; Ellesmere only after *signe*.

The reading of line 230 of Hengwrt does not permit an iambic reading: that of Ellesmere does:

Hengwrt: He may nat weepe / thogh þat he soore smerte
Ellesmere: He may nat wepe / al thogh hym soore smerte
Add. 5140:   He may nat wepe / thowe he sore smert

We shall never know which was Chaucer's form, although I should incline to the Hengwrt because of the trochaic rhythm after the virga.

Certainly the reading of lines 323–327 is more subtle in the Hengwrt and the intonation pattern more clearly indicated:

Hengwrt: In termes / hadde he caas / and doomes alle
             That from tyme of Kyng William / weere falle
             Ther to / he koude endite / and make a thyng
             Ther koude no wight pynchen at his writyng
             And every statut . koude he pleyn by roote
Ellesmere   In termes hadde he caas and doomes alle
             That from the tyme / of Kyng William were yfalle
             Ther to / he koude endite and make a thyng
             Ther koude no wight / pynchen at his writyng
             And every statut / koude he pleyn by rote
Add. 5140:   In termis hadde he cas / and domys alle
             That fro the tyme of King William were falle
             Thereto he cowde endyte and make a thyng
             Ther cowde no wyht / pynche at his writyng
             And every statute / cowde he pleyn be roote

The slight pauses after *termes* and *cas*; after *William* rather than after *tyme*; and after *endite* enhance the conversational quality.

In the description of the Frankelyn, Hengwrt indicates at least fourteen junctures not indicated in Ellesmere.

Hengwrt: Wo was his cook / but if his sauce weere
             Poynaunt / and sharp / and redy al his geere
Ellesmere has no virga after *cook* or after *poynaunt*.

Hengwrt: At sessions / ther was he / lord and sire
             fful ofte tyme / he was knyght of the shire

Ellesmere has no marks of punctuation whatever; Additional 5140 follows Hengwrt.

Or, notice the pointing in the description of the Haberdasher *et alia*:

Hengwrt: fful fressh and newe / hir geere apyked was
            Hir knyves weere chaped / noght with bras
            But al with silver / wroght ful cleene and wel
            Hir girdles and hir pouches / everydel
            Wel seemed eech of hem / a fair burgeys
            To sitten in a yeldehalle / on a deys
            Everych / for the wisdom / þat he kan
            Was shaply / for to been an alderman
            ffor Catel / hadde they ynogh / and rente
            And eek hir wyves / wolde it wel assente

                                                    (*Prol.* 366–374)

Ellesmere has only one mark of punctuation in the entire passage, after *hem* in *wel semed ech of hem / a fair burgeys*. Additional 5140 more nearly accords with Hengwrt, although there are five omissions and two occasions where the intonation would differ: *Hir knyves were nat / chaped wt bras* and *Was shaply for to been / an alderman*.

Or, in the description of the Cook. The absence of all pointing except after *seethe*, *mortreaux*, and *blankmanger*, makes it possible to scan the description iambically, but if the reader heeds the significance of the virga in the Hengwrt such a scansion is impossible:

            A cook they hadde with hem / for the nones
            To boille the chiknes / with the Marybones
            And poudre marchaunt . tart / and / galyngale
            Wel koude he knowe / a draghte of London ale
            He koude rooste / and seethe / and broille / and frye
            Maken morteux / and wel bake a pye
            But great harm was it / as it thoughte me
            That on his shyne / a mormal hadde he
            ffor blankmanger / that maade he with the beste

                                                    (*Prol.* 379–387)

Additional 5140 lends support to the hypothesis that at least the scribe did not think of an iambic pattern by his text of line 383: *He coude rost and seth / boyle and frye.* Line 385 reads: *But greet harm was it / as thought me,* and the scribe omits the *that* in line 387.

In character sketch after character sketch the pointing of Hengwrt is more subtle and more conversational than that of the Ellesmere.

What is true of the *Prologue* is also true of the *Tales* themselves. Unless he is working with the original MSS. the investigator must guard against the failure of microfilms and the Xerox copies made from them to register the marks of punctuation. In my copy of the Ellesmere *Pardoner's Tale*, for example, the marks are not visible although the space between the words would indicate that perhaps a mark might appear on the original. Even so, however, the pointing of the Hengwrt is more subtle, although the general agreement is very close. The Hengwrt pointing is fuller than that of the Ellesmere. The scribe of the Hengwrt places, in line 289, a virga after *cherl*; but not he of the Ellesmere. The presence of the virga would place a greater stress on the *and*; moreover it would prevent any tendency to read the line as iambic:

$$/ \quad \times \times / \quad / \quad / \times / \quad / \times$$
This was a fals cherl / and a fals justice

Rhythmically the line ends on a *cursus planus*.

Rarely does the scribe of Ellesmere point more fully than he of the Hengwrt, but two lines from the *Pardoner's Tale* are rather interesting, lines 294 and 303:

Wherfore I seye / al day / as men may see
But nathelees / passe over / is no fors.

Hengwrt has no mark after *sey* nor *nathelees*, nor does the additional mark of Ellesmere really add anything. But in line 363, the pointing of Hengwrt is better than that of the Ellesmere:

Wal every wike / er þt the cok hym croweth
ffastynge / drynken of this well a draghte . . .

A virga after *drynken* instead of after *ffastynge* fails to make sense. It could be an example of the type of ' mismetering ' about which Chaucer complained to Adam.

On the other hand, the scribe of the Ellesmere achieves a slightly different effect than he of the Hengwrt by his double pointing of line 374. A modern editor prints the line without any pointing, makes it possible to scan the line as iambic, but takes away the subtle effect:

Robinson: He shal have multipliyng of his grayn
Ellesmere: He shal have / multipliyng/ of his grayn
Hengwrt: He shal have / multiplyyng of his grayn

Granted that the difference is subtle, from iambic, to trochaic, to a modified *tardus*.

Often the textual differences between the Ellesmere and the Hengwrt are slight enough to disturb the iambic hypothesis, but have no effect on the basic rhythmical pattern controlled by the virga. In line 422 we have *seme* in Hengwrt, *semen* in Ellesmere; in line 430, *make* and *maken*, line 468, *ete* and *eten*. The scribe of the Hengwrt regularly omits the ' n '—*telle* (820), *bitwixe* (832), *ete*, *dronke* (863), etc. Or, take line 578. Ellesmere reads ' Looketh the Bible and ther ye may it leere ' which can be scanned as iambic, but in Hengwrt it reads, ' Looketh the Bible / and ther ye may leere,' which cannot. Line 589 of Ellesmere reads 'And now I have spoken of glotonye ' which cannot be scanned as iambic, but since Hengwrt can more nearly be scanned so—'And now / that I have spoken of glotonye '—the modern editor adopts Hengwrt. Actually, however, the line ends in a *cursus tardus*— / × × / × ×.

Line 863 is manifestly inferior in Hengwrt to that in Ellesmere. Robinson adopts Ellesmere; Donaldson, Hengwrt, although without the subtle suggestion of intonation which the MS. provides:

Ellesmere: That eten or dronken hath / of this confiture
Hengwrt: That ete / or dronk / hath of this confiture

Both readings of line 873 are good. Ten Brink would, of course, have emended both.

Ellesmere: The thridde he kepte clene / for his owene drynke
Hengwrt: The thridde / he kepte clene for his drynke

Since by giving an ' archaic ' pronunciation to *kepte* and *clene* the line can be forced into an iambic pattern, modern editors adopt Hengwrt. The same is true of line 880:

Ellesmere: ffor right so / as they hadde cast his deeth bifoore
Hengwrt: ffor right as they / hadde cast his deeth bifore

It is true, of course, that a scribe can make mistakes when copying, or when writing from dictation, but we must remember that there was careful supervision over the scribe. There are many instances in both Hengwrt and Ellesmere where the scribe, having missed a word, has inserted it. It is time that we recognize that the Chaucerian investigators of the nineteenth century took a romantic attitude toward their subject, that they formulated hypotheses that have proved untenable, that they jumped to unwarranted conclusions. It is time that Chaucerians stop the widely current professorial practice of rationalization and be willing to discard the ideas imposed upon them by their masters when they were graduate students. As Whitehead has said: ' Success is never absolute, and progress in the right direction is the result of a slow, gradual process of continual comparison of ideas with facts.' Further investigators will unearth facts that will probably alter some of the conclusions at which I have arrived. There is much to be done, much debris to be cleared away, and many new ideas to be formulated. With modern methods for providing the scholar with his materials for research, the possibilities are great. Just as an art critic cannot arrive at a final judgment about a painting from photographs, a literary scholar cannot arrive at a final judgment about a MS. from a photograph. He should be careful to check his findings in the light of the original.

More than ever the truth of Sir William McCormick's statement to Manley becomes evident. He would be doing a greater service to Chaucerian scholarship, Sir William told Manly, if he were to edit two of the best MSS. than to attempt to reconstruct the archetype. We must remember that Child, Kittredge, Manly, Robinson, Root and others began their work on the unsubstantiated hypothesis that Chaucer—unique and quite apart from the stream of the tradition— wrote iambic pentameter. There is pathos, therefore, in Manly's realization after his laborious task was complete that Chaucer's versification was not so regular as had been supposed and that a restudy of his prosody was in order; but a restudy impossible except by a re-examination of the MSS. themselves.

I find wholly naive the conception that for the sake of meter Chaucer clung to an archaic pronunciation. Human nature has not changed since Chaucer's day, nor have the practices of poets, the most human of us all.

CHAPTER IV

CHAUCER'S DISCIPLES

I mentioned at the outset that one of the basic truths about poets and poetry is that a contemporary disciple of the poet is ' expected to have and probably does have a clear understanding of the basic characteristics of the work of his master.' He will not, however, ever capture the subtly unique quality of the master. Hoccleve spoke of Chaucer as his master, and scholars have in general granted his claim. Having granted it, however, they proceed to make of him a completely tone-deaf poetaster. I maintain that the basic rhythmical pattern will be more apparent in a disciple than in the subtler work of the master. The imitators of Spenser, of Milton, of Pope furnish abundant examples. Why then, not the imitators of Chaucer?

Do the Hoccleve MSS. lend support to the hypothesis I have presented? Certain MSS. of the *Regement of Princes*, except for spelling, tell us nothing. Others, however, tell us much. They reveal all too clearly that Furnivall's attack on Hoccleve was unwarranted. Furnivall (*Hoccleve's Works*, 1892, I–xl–xlii (*passim*)) said of Hoccleve that his ' meter is poor; so long as he can count ten syllables by his fingers, he is content; ' that ' he constantly thwarts the natural run of his line by putting stress on a word that shouldn't bear it, or using a strong syllable as a weak one; ' that ' he turns the pronoun *hire*, her, into two syllables; ' that he ' often breaks a measure awkwardly with his pause; ' of that ' he not only lets the metrical pause stop the cutting-off of a final *e* before a vowel or an *H*, but he keeps the *e* also in other parts of the one.' These are serious charges to bring against a poet with Hoccleve's standing among his contemporaries, and not flattering to his host of readers.

Space does not permit a review of Furnivall's treatment of Harleian 4866, a good MS. of the *Regement of Princes*, which he chose to edit. Suffice it to say that in the first hundred lines he added twenty-four final *e*'s in order to make the verses iambic decasyllabic; and where that wouldn't do, he substituted readings from another MS.

Harleian's	Which that this world / hath ay on honde	1.2
becomes in Furnivall	Which that this troubly world hath ay on honde	
Harleian's	My tremlyng hert so gret gastnesse hadde	1.20

becomes in Furnivall My tremblyng hert so gretë gastenesse hadde
Harleian's   Myn hert made to myn tributarie   1.80
becomes in Furnivall Myn hert [e] madë to hym tributarie
and so on.

The following stanza is from the *Regement of Princes* as amended
by Furnivall.

> Thus ilkë nyught I walwyd to and fro,
> Sekyng restë; but certeynly sche
> Apperrid noght, for þoght, my crewel fo,
> Chaced hadde hir & slepe a-way fro me;
> And for I schuldë not allonë be.
> Agayn my luste; Wach profrid his seruise,
> And I admitted hym in hevy wyse.

At least Furnivall no longer believed final -*e* in rhyme pronounced.
When we consult the MSS., however, what do we find? The story is
quite different. Here is the same stanza 11 from Oxford Bodleian
Douce 158:

> This ilk nyght I walwed to and fro
> Sechyng rest / but certenly she
> apperid not / for þogh my cruel foo
> hadde chaced her / and slep a way fro mee
> And for I should not allone bee
> Ageyn my lust wache profred hir seruyse
> And I admitted hym in heui wyse.

In *De Regimine Principum*, Arundel MS. 38, the marks of punctuation begin on f 2ʳ with a *virga* (/). In the last stanza on f 2 we find
a *punctus elevatus* (√).

> The smert of thouʒt . and by expience

In the succeeding folios he uses the *virga* (/), the *punctus elevatus* (√),
occasionally the *double virga* (/ /), and occasionally the low *punctum*
(.). It would be difficult to say that these marks invariably meant
what they earlier did. In any case, they indicate the structures. The
scribe of Harleian 4866 placed a *virga* (/) after *reste* and a high
punctum (·) after *luste*. *þoght* is the reading of Harleian 4866, but
þogh is that of Oxford Bodl. Douce 158 and B. M. Sloane MS. 1212.

Let us, however, look a little more carefully at the *Regement of
Princes* in Bodl. Ashmole 189. This is a beautiful MS., very carefully
written, and carefully punctuated. The *virga* (/) occurs internally

and a *punctum circumflexus* (,[1]) at the end of every line unless the sense carries over to the following line, in which case there is no punctuation. The following are stanzas 280–283 in ' Comendacion of Chaucer ':

> With herte tremblings / as the leef of aspe,
> Ffadir sith ye me rede to do so,
> Of my simple conceit / wol I the claspe,
> Un do / and lete hit / at his large goo,
> But welawey / so is myn herte woo,
> That the honour / of Englissh toñge is deed,
> Of wiche I wonte was / have counseil and reed,
>
> O my maister deere / and fadir reverent,
> Mi maister Chaucer floure of eloquence,
> Mirrour of fructuous entendement
> O universel / fadir in science,
> Allas þat þow / thin excellent prudence,
> In thi bedde mortal / mi ʒte nouʒt biquethe,
> What eiled deth / allas whi wolde he sle the,
>
> O deeth þou didest not harme singulere,
> In slauʒtir of him / but al this londe smertith
> But netheles / ʒit hast þou no powere,
> His name slee / his hiʒe vertu a stirtith,
> Unslain of the / wiche ay us lifly hertith,
> With bookes / of his ordinat enditings,
> That is to al this lande / enlumynynge,   Stanzas 280–282

Quite obviously one can torture most of the foregoing into an iambic pattern if he disregards the position of the virga, pronounces final *e*'s and makes substitutions of trochees and anapests for iambs. Although not great poetry, however read, it has a simple sincerity if one reads it rhythmically and observes the single bar juncture at the virga. There is no subtlety in the verse it is true, but a contemporary reader would find nothing strange in its movement. But although it has no real inner subtlety it is an obvious imitation. The verse makes extensive use of the *cursus* or of *cadences*. The first of the foregoing stanzas contains no example of the classic *cursus* but several echoes of the classic *cursus* as modified by the stressed endings

---

[1] The actual mark of punctuation is not the same as our comma. It is a heavy period with a swirling very light comet's tail.

common in English. Line 1 is such a one (/ / × × × / × /): *herte tremblyng | as the leef of aspe*; line 2 is a *tardus: me rede to do so*; lines 3, 4, and 7 a modified *planus* (/ × × /): *wol I the claspe, at his large goo, counseil and reed*; 5 is a modified *trochaicus* (/ × / × /): *so is myn herte woo*.

The second of the foregoing stanzas, however, contains examples of the classical *cursus*. Line 1, 2 3 are *tardus: and fadir reverent, floure of eloquence, fructuous entendement*; 4, 5, and 7 are the *planus: fadir in science, excellent prudence, whi wolde he sle the*; 6 is a modified *planus* (/ × × /): *mizte nouzt biquethe*. In the third of the foregoing stanzas the first six line endings are *cursus planus*, and seven is a slightly modified *tardus*.

I did not select these stanzas because of their rhythyms but because of their tribute to Chaucer. It is obvious, however, that Hoccleve by imitating Chaucer's *verses of cadence* better understood the nature of Chaucer's prosody than did Furnivall who thought him metrically incompetent.

When we turn to Lydgate, who has indeed received more than his share of abuse, we find the subtleties of cadence almost forgotten. There are traces of it, but not in the way we find it in Hoccleve. I make no elaborate claims for Lydgate, but let us look on one of the MSS., the very beautiful ' aureate ' MS. of his *Life of St. Edmund* (Harl. 2278 Plut.). The scribe of this exquisite MS., filled with illuminations of great artistic excellence, was most careful with his punctuation, the *virga* (/). If the reader observes this mark remembering that it is the same as the single bar juncture of the modern linguistic scholars, he will discover that there are no sing-song nor broken-backed lines. True, he will not find great poetry either, but he will find competent versification. In the second stanza Lydgate invokes the aid of St. Edmund:

> Now glorious martir / of Bury chief patron
> In Saxonie born / of the blood roial
> Conveie my mater / be my proteccioun
> Sithe in thi support / myn hope abideth al
> Directe my penne / of that I write shal
> ffor so thi favour / fro me not ne twynne
> Upon the story / thus I will be gynne.

The story then moves in an easy manner, not to be lightly regarded. If the reader heeds the marks of punctuation, he will discover that

Lydgate has achieved an easy conversational style. The following stanza, for example, has a pleasant movement:

> First in his armys / he gan him to embrace
> And seide Emond my neuew most entier
> My wil is this / er I parte fro this place
> And will also / that alle men it heere
> Because thow hast maad me so good cheere
> What euer falle / of myn ageyn komyng
> Or I departe / receyve of me this ryng.

In the first of the two stanzas, we have the *planus* in lines 1, 2, and 5; the *tardus* in 3, and a crude modification in line 5. Four is iambic. The second stanza contains none.

I think it is apparent that although Gascoigne's analysis of Chaucer's verse and that of his contemporaries was crude, as was also that of G. F. Nott, they were nearer a correct understanding of its nature than were the 19 C. scholars who read his verses as essentially iambic. But it is also obvious that I have done no more than to open the door to a realistic study of Chaucerian prosody, a study long overdue.

In the foregoing discussion of the nature of Chaucer's prosody I have attempted to give evidence for the outline of Chaucer's development that I have roughly sketched. Much remains to be done, but it is the work for many rather than for one. We must realize that the iambic basis for Chaucer's prosody was a hypothesis and only that and that we need to begin anew. We must bear in mind certain characteristics of the English used by Chaucer in his verse—the same characteristics that we find in his prose: final unaccented -e was *not* sounded, stress accents had become relatively fixed, the punctuation marks were essentially intonational guides.

It is possible to trace Chaucer's development from the stiff verse of the *Boke of the Duches*, through his *verses of cadence*, such as the *ABC*, the fusion of two styles in the *Hous of Fame*, to the mature works where he has caught the speech rhythms of his age—speech rhythms and vocabulary which were essentially those of the audience to which he addressed himself. It would do less than justice to Chaucer to speak of the prosody of *The Legend of Good Women*, *Troilus and Criseyde*, and the *Canterbury Tales* as being alike. The exigencies of the stanza form and of the story itself of the *Troilus* scarcely permit the subtle rhythmic variations that one finds in the *Canterbury Tales* dictated by the character of the speakers. Scholars have long been aware, of course, of the superiority of certain tales, but I doubt if under existing ideas of his prosody, they could possibly appreciate the manifold subtleties of the different styles in the *Pardoner's Tale* in which Chaucer so magnificently captures the pulpit tones of the Pardoner as well as those of his ordinary conversation when speaking to the pilgrims.

Chaucer's mature style is the perfect distillation of the speech of his England—that of the urbane, sophisticated court of Richard II; that speech reflecting the strong influence of ecclesiastic writing and sermoning; that of persons who have steeped themselves in popular romances; that of the court, the counting house, the village, and the field. His great achievement lies in the artistry with which in his poetry he has eradicated the prolixity of daily speech without sacrificing its rhythms.

His magnificent ear has caught the subtle gradations of tone of social degree and individual calling in his couplets as well as in the intricate *rime royal* stanzas. The marks of punctuation indicate these rhythms and intonations, and an examination of the MSS. of his disciples reveal that they understood his prosody. We should, therefore, recognize that the iambic decasyllabic theory of poetry has no place in the discussion of English poetry until the humanistic revival in the sixteenth century. If we do this the entire history of English prosody will appear both clearer and more logical than it does at the present.

APPENDIX

The myry talkyng of the hoost / to the
Phisician and the Pardoner

Oure hoost gan to swere / as he were wood
Harrow quod he / by nayles and by blood
This was a fals cherl / and a fals justise
As shameful deeth / as herte may devyse   290
Come to thise Juges / and hir advocatȝ
Algate this sely mayde / is slayn allas
Allas / to deere boghte she beautee
Wherfore I sey alday / þt men may se
That yiftes of ffortune / and of nature   295
Been cause of deeth / to many a creature
Of bothe yiftes / þt I speke of now
Men han ful ofte / moore for harm than prow   300
But trewely / myn owene maister deere
This is a pitous tale / for to heere
But nathelees passe over / is no fors
I pray to god / so save thy gentil cors
And eek thyne urinals / and thy jurdones   305
Thyn ypocras / and eek thy galyones
And every boyste / ful of thy letuarie
God blesse hem / and oure lady Seinte Marie
So mote I then / thow art a propre man
And lyk a prelat / by Seint Ronyan   310
Seyde I nat wel / I kan nat speke in terme
But wel I woot / thow doost myn herte to erme
That I almoost / have caught / a cardynacle
By corpus bones / but if I have triacle
Or ellis a draghte / of moyste and corny ale   315
Or but I heere anon / a murye tale
Myn herte is lost / for pitee of this mayde
Thow beel amy / thow pardoner he sayde
Tel us som myrthe / or japes right anon
It shal be doon quod he / by Seint Ronyon   320
But first quod he / heere at this ale stake

I wol bothe drynke / and eten of a cake
And right anon / thise gentils gonne to crye
Nay lat hym telle us / of no ribawdye
Tel us som moral thyng / þt we may leere   325
Som wit / and thanne wol we gladly heere
I graunte y wis quod he / but I moot thynke
Upon som honeste thyng / whil þt I drynke   328
Radix omnium malorum / est cupiditas / / ad Thimotheum 6°

Here bigynneth the prologe of the Pardoners tale

Lordynges quod he / in chirches whan I preche
I peyne me / to han an hauteyn speche   330
And rynge it out / as round as gooth a belle
ffor I kan / al by rote that I telle
My theme is alwey oon / and ever was
Radix malorum / est cupiditas
Ffirst I pronounce / whennes þt I come   335
And thanne my bulles / shewe I alle and some
Oure lige lordes seel / on my patente
That shewe I first / my body to warente
That no man be so boold / ne preest ne clerk
Me to destourbe / of Cristes holy werk   340
And after that / thanne telle I forth my tales
Bulles of Popes / and of cardynales
Of patriarkes / and bisshopes I shewe
And in latyn / I speke a wordes fewe
To saffron with / my predicacioun   345
And for to stire hem / to devocioun
Thanne shewe I forth / my longe cristal stones
Ycrammed ful / of cloutes and of bones
Relikes been they / as wenen they echon
Thanne have I in a latoun / a shulder bon   350
Which þt was / of an holy Jewes sheep
Goode men I seye / tak of my wordes keep
If þt this boon be wasshe / in any welle
If cow / or calf / or sheep / or oxe swelle
That any worm hath ete / or worm ystonge   355
Taak water of that welle / and wassh his tonge
And it is hool anoon / and forthermoor
Of pokkes / and of scabbe / and every soor

Shal every sheep be hool / þt of this welle
Drynketh a draughte / taak keepe eek what I telle   360
If þt the goode man / þt the bestes oweth
Wol every wike / er þt the cok hym croweth
ffastynge / drynken of this welle a draghte
As thilke holy Jew / oure eldres taghte
Hise bestes and his stoor / shal multiplie   365
And sire also / it heeleth jalousie
ffor thogh a man / be falle in jalous rage
Lat maken with this water / his potage
And nevere shal he moore / his wyf mystriste
Thogh he the soothe / of hir defaute wiste   370
Al hadde she / taken preestes / two or thre
Heere is a miteyn eek / þt ye may se
He þt his hand / wol putte / in this mitayn
He shal have / multiplyyng of his grayn
Whan he hath sowen / be it whete or otes   375
So þt / he / offre pens / or ellis grotes
Goode men and wommen / o thyng warne I yow
If any wight / be in this chirche now
That hath don synne horrible / that he
Dar nat for shame / of it yshriven be   380
Or any womman / be she yong or old
That hath ymaked / hir housbond cokewold
Swich folk / shal have no power / ne no grace
To offren to my relikes / in this place
And who so fyndeth hym / out of swich blame   385
He wol come up / and offre a goddes name
And I assoille hym / by the auctoritee
Which þt by bulle / ygraunted was to me
By this gaude / have I wonne / yeer by yeer
An hundred mark / sith I was pardoner   390
I stonde lyk a clerk / in my pulpet
And whan þt lewed peple / is doun yset
I preche so / as ye han herd bifore
And telle / an hundred false japes more
Thanne peyne I me / to strecche forth the nekke   395
And Est and West / up on the peple I bekke
As dooth a dowve / sittyng on a berne
Myne handes / and my tonge goon so yerne

G

That it is joye / to se my bisynesse
Of avarice / and of swich cursednesse   400
Is al my prechyng / for to make hem free
To yeven hir pens / and namely un to me
ffor myn entente is nat / but for to wynne
And no thyng / for correcioun of synne
I rekke never / whan þt they ben beryed   405
Thogh þt hir soules / goon a blakeberyed
ffor certes / many a predicacioun
Comth ofte tyme / of yvel entencioun
Som for plesance of folk / and flaterye
To been avanced / by ypocrisie   410
And som for veyne glorie / and som for hate
ffor when I dar / noon oother weyes debate
Thanne wol I stynge hym / with my tonge smerte
In prechyng / so þt he shal nat asterte
To been diffamed falsly / if þt he   415
Hath trespased / to my bretheren / or to me
ffor though I telle noght / his propre name
Men shal wel knowe / that it is the same
By signes / and by othere circumstances
Thus quyte I folk / that doon us displesances   420
Thus spete I ought / my venym under hewe
Of holynesse / to seme holy and trewe
But shortly / myn entente I wol devyse
I preche of no thyng / but for coveitise
Therfore my theme is yet / and ever was   425
Radix malorum / est cupiditas
Thus kan I preche / agayn that same vice
Which þt I use / and that is avarice
But though my self be gilty in that synne
Yet kan I make / oother folk to twynne   430
ffrom avarice / and soore to repente
But that is nat / my principal entente
I preche no thyng / but for coveitise
Of this matere / it oghte ynow suffise
Thanne telle I hem / ensamples many oon   435
Of olde stories / longe tyme agoon
ffor lewed peple / loven tales olde
Swiche thynges / kan they wel reporte and holde

What trow ye / þt whiles I may preche
And wynne / gold and silver / for I teche   440
That I wol lyve in poverte / wilfully
Nay nay / I thoghte it never trewely
ffor I wol preche / and begge / in sondry landes
I wol nat do no labour / with myne handes
Ne make baskettes / and lyve ther by   445
By cause / I wol nat beggen ydelly
I wol none of the Apostles countrefete
I wol have moneye / wolle / chese / and whete
Al were it yeven / of the poverest page
Or of the povereste widwe / in a village   450
Al sholde hir children / sterve for famyne
Nay I wol drynke / licour of the vyne
And have a ioly wenche / in every toun
But herkneth lordynges / in conclusioun
Youre likyng is / þt I shal telle a tale   455
Now have I dronke / a draghte of corny ale
By god I hope / I shal yow telle a thyng
That shal by resoun / been at youre likyng
ffor thogh my self be / a ful vicious man
A moral tale / yet I yow telle kan   460
Which I am wont to preche / for to wynne
Now holde youre pees / my tale I wol bigynne   462

Here bigynneth the pardoners tale

In fflandres / whilom was a compaignye
Of yonge folk / that haunteden folye
As riot / hasard / stewes / and tavernes   465
Where as with harpes / lutes / and gyternes
They daunce / and pleyen at dees / bothe day and nyght
And ete also and drynke / over hir myght
Thurgh which / they doon the devel sacrifise
With inne that develes temple / in cursed wise   470
By superfluytee / abhomynable
Hir othes been so grete / and so dampnable
That it is grisly / for to heere hem swere
Oure blissed lordes body / they to tere
Hem thoughte / that Jewes / rente hym noght ynough 475
And eech of hem / at otheres synne lough

And right anon / thanne coomen Tombesteres
ffetys and smale / and yonge ffrutesteres
Syngeris with harpes / baudes / wavfereres
Whiche been / the verray develes officers   480
To kyndle and blowe / the fyr of lecherye
That is annexed / un to glotonye
The holy writ take I / to my witnesse
That luxure / is in wyn / and dronkenesse
Lo how þt dronken loth / unkyndely   485
Lay by his doghtres two / unwityngly
So dronke he was / he nyste what he wroghte
Herodes / who so wel the stories soghte
Whan he of wyn was replet / at his feste
Right at his owene table / he yaf his heste   490
To sleen the Baptist John / ful giltelees
Senec / seith a good word doutelees
He seith / he kan no difference fynde
Bitwix a man / that is out of his mynde
And a man / which þt is dronkelewe   495
But that woodnesse / yfallen in a sherewe
Persevereth lenger / than dooth dronkenesse
O glotonye / ful of cursednesse
O cause first / of oure confusioun
O original / of oure dampnacioun   500
Til Crist hadde boght us / with his blood agayn
Lo how deere / shortly for to sayn
Aboght was / thilke cursed vileynye
Corrupt / was al this world for glotonye
Adam oure fader / and his wyf also   505
ffro Paradys / to labour and to wo
Were dryven for that vice / it is no drede
ffor whil þt Adam fasted / as I rede
He was in Paradys / and whan þt he
Eet of the frut / defended on a tree   510
Anon he was out cast / to wo and peyne
O glotonye / on thee wel oghte us pleyne
O wiste a man / how many maladies
ffolwen of excesse / and of glotonyes
He wolde been / the moore mesurable   515
Of his diete / sittyng at his table

Allas the shorte throte / the tendre mouth
Maketh / þt Est / and West / and North and South
In erthe / in eyr / in water / men to swinke
To gete a gloton / deyntee mete and drynke   520
Of this matere / O Paul / wel kanstow trete
Mete un to wombe / and wombe eek un to mete
Shal god destroyen bothe / as Paulus seith
Allas a foul thyng / is it by my feith   .
To seye this word / and fouler is the dede   525
Whan man so drynketh / of the white and rede
That of his throte / he maketh his pryvee
Thurgh / thilke cursed superfluite
The apostle wepyng / seith ful pitously
Ther walken manye / of whiche yow toold have I   530
I seye it now wepyng / with pitous voys
Ther been enemys / of Cristes croys
Of whiche the ende is deth/wombe is hir god
O wombe / o bely / o stynkyng cod
ffulfilled of dong / and of corrupcioun   535
At either ende of thee / foul is the soun
How greet labour / and cost / is thee to fynde
Thise cokes / how they stampe / and streyne / and grynde
And turnen substance / in to accident
To fulfillen al / the likerous talent   540
Out of the harde bones / knokke they
The mary / for they caste nat awey
That may go thurgh the golet / softe and soote
Of spicerie / of lief / and bark / and roote
Shal been his sauce / ymaked by delit   545
To make hym yet / a newer appetit
But certes / he that haunteth swiche delices
Is deed / whil þt he lyveth in tho vices
A lecherous thyng is wyn / / and dronkenesse
Is ful of stryvyng / and of wrecchednesse   550
O dronke man / disfigured is thy face
Sour is thy breeth / foul artow to embrace
And thurgh thy dronke nose / semeth the soun
As thogh thou seydest ay / Sampsoun Sampsoun
And yet god woot / Sampson drank nevere no wyn   555
Thou fallest / as it were a stiked swyn

Thy tonge is lost / and al thyn honest cure
ffor dronkenesse / is verray sepulture
Of mannes wit / and his distrecioun
In whom þt drynke / hath domynacioun   560
He kan no conseil kepe / it is no drede
Now kepe yow / fro the white and fro the rede
And namely / fro the white wyn of Lepe
That is to selle / in ffisshstrete / or in Chepe
This wyn of Spaigne / crepeth subtilly   565
In othere wynes / growynge faste by
Of which / ther riseth swich fumositee
That whan a man / hath dronken draghtes thre
And weneth þt he be / at hom in Chepe
He is in Spaigne / right at the toune of Lepe   570
Nat at the Rochel / ne at Burdeux toun
And thanne wol he seyn / Sampson Sampsoun
But herkneth lordynges / o word I yow preye
That alle the sovereyn actes / dar I seye
Of victories / in the olde testament   575
Thurgh verray god / that is omnipotent
Were doon in abstinence / and in prayere
Looketh the Bible / and ther ye may it leere
Looke Attilla / the grete conquerour
Deyde in his sleep / with shame and dishonour   580
Bledyng at his nose / in dronkenesse
A capitayn / shold lyve in sobrenesse
And over al this / avyseth yow right wel
What was comaunded / un to Lamwel
Nat Samuel / but Lamwel seye I   585
Redeth the Bible / and fynd it expresly
Of wyn yevynge / to hem þt han justise
Namoore of this / for it may wel suffise
And now / that I have spoken of glotonye
Now wol I / yow defende hasardrye   590
Hasard / is verray moder of lesynges
And of deceite / and cursed forswerynges
Blaspheme of Crist / manslaughtre / and wast / also
Of catel / and of tyme / and forthermo
It is reprove / and contrarie of honour   595
ffor to ben holden / a commune hasardour

And evere the hyer / he is of estaat
The moore is he holden desolat
If þt a prynce / useth hasardrye
In alle governance / and policye   600
He is / as by commune opynyoun
Yholde / the lasse in reputacioun
Stilbon / that was a wys embassadour
Was sent to Corynthe / in ful gret honour
ffro Lacedómye / to make hire alliaunce   605
And whan he cam / hym happed perchaunce
That alle the gretteste / þt were of that lond
Pleiynge at the hasard / he hem fond
ffor which as soone / as it myghte be
He stal hym hom agayn / to his contree   610
And seyde / ther wol I nat lese my name
Ny wol nat take on me / so greet defame
Yow for to allie / un to none hasardours
Sendeth / othere wise embassadours
ffor by my trouthe / me were levere dye   615
Than I yow sholde / to hasardours allye
ffor ye that been / so glorious in honours
Shal nat allye yow / with hasardours
As by my wyl / ne as by my tretee
This wise philosophre / thus seyde he   620
Looke eek / that to the kyng Demetrius
The kyng of Parthes / as the book seith us
Sente hym a paire of dees / of gold in scorn
ffor he hadde used / hasard ther biforn
ffor which / he heeld his glorie / or his renoun 625
At no value / or reputacioun
Lordes may fynden / oother manere pley
Honeste ynow / to dryve the day awey
Now wol I speke / of oothes false and grete
A word or two / as olde bokes trete   630
Greet sweryng / is a thyng abhomynable
And fals sweryng / is yet moore reprenable
The heighe god / forbad sweryng at al
Witnesse on Mathew / but in special
Of sweryng / seith the holy Jeremye   635
Thow shalt swere sooth thyne othes / and nat lye

And swere in doom / and eek in rightwisnesse
But ydel sweryng / is a cursednesse
Bihoold and se / þt in the firste table
Of heighe goddes hestes honurable   640
How þt the seconde heste of hym / is this
Take nat my name / in ydel or amys
Lo rather he forbedeth / swich sweryng
Than homycide / or many a cursed thyng
I seye / þt as by ordre / thus it standeth   645
This knoweth / that hise hestes understandeth
How that the seconde heste of god / is that
And forther over / I wol thee telle al plat
That vengeance / shal nat parten from his hous
That of hise othes / is to outrageous   650
By goddes precious herte / and by his nayles
And by the blood of Crist / that is in hayles
Sevene is my chance / and thyn is cynk and treye
By goddes armes / if thow falsly pleye
This dagger / shal thurgh out thyn herte go   655
This frut cometh / of the bicche bones two
fforsweryng / ire / falsnesse / homycide
Now for the love of Crist / that for us dyde
Lete youre othes / bothe grete and smale
But sires / now wol I / telle forth my tale   660
Thise riotours thre / of whiche I telle
Longe erst / er pryme ronge of any belle
Were set hem / in a taverne to drynke
And as they sat / they herde a belle klynke
Biforn a cors / was caryed to his grave   665
That oon of hem / gan callen to his knave
Go bet quod he / and axe redily
What cors is this / that passeth heer forby
And looke / þt thow reporte his name wel
Sire quod this boy / it nedeth never a del   670
It was me told / er ye cam heer two houres
He was pardee / an old felawe of youres
And sodeynly / he was yslayn to nyght
ffordronke / as he sat on his bench upright
Ther cam a privee theef / men clepeth deeth   675
That in this contree / al the peple sleeth

And with his spere / he smoot his herte atwo
And wente his wey / with outen wordes mo
He hath / a thousand slayn this pestilence
And maister / er ye come in his presence   680
Me thynketh / that it were necessarie
ffor to be war / of swich an adversarie
Beeth redy / for to meete hym evermoore
Thus taughte me my dame / I seye namoore
By Seinte Marie / seyde this Taverner   685
The child seith sooth / for he hath slayn this yer
Henne over a myle / withinne a greet village
Bothe man and womman / child and hyne and page
I trowe / his habitacioun be there
To been avysed / greet wisdom it were   690
Er that he dide / a man a dishonour
Ye goddes armes / quod this riotour
Is it swich peril / with hym for to meete
I shal hym seke / by way / and eek by strete
I make avow / to goddes digne bones   695
Herkneth felawes / we thre been alones
Lat ech of us / holde up his hand to oother
And ech of us / bicome ootheres brother
And we wol sleen / this false traytour deeth
He shal be slayn / he þt so manye sleeth   700
By goddes dignytee / er it be nyght
Togidres han thise thre / hir trouthes plyght
To lyve and dyen / ech of hem with oother
As thogh he were / his owene ybore brother
And up they stirte / al dronken / in this rage   705
And forth they goon / towardes that village
Of which the taverner / hadde spoke biforn
And many a grisly ooth / thanne han they swom
And Cristes blessed body / they torente
Deeth shal be deed / if they may hym hente   710
Whan they han goon / nat fully half a myle
Right as they wolde / han treden over a style
An old man and a poure / with hem mette
This olde man / ful mekely hem grette
And seyde thus / now lordes god yow se   715
The proudeste / of thise riotours thre

Answerde agayn / what carl wt sory grace
Why artow al forwrapped / save thy face
Why lyvestow so longe / in so greet age
This olde man / gan looke in his visage   720
And seyde thus / for I ne kan nat fynde
A man / thogh þt I walked in to Inde
Neither in citee / ne in no village
That wolde chaunge / his youthe for myn age
And therfore moot I han / myn age stille   725
As longe tyme / as it is goddes wille
Ne deeth allas / ne wol nat have my lyf
Thus walke I / lyk a resteless caytyf
And on the ground / which is my modres gate
I knokke with my staf / bothe erly and late   730
And seye / leeve moder leet me in
Lo how I vanysshe / flessh and blood and skyn
Allas / whan shal my bones / been at reste
Moder / with yow / wolde I chaunge my cheste
That in my chambre / longe tyme hath be   735
Ye for an heyre clowt / to wrappe me
But yet to me / she wol nat / do that grace
ffor which ful pale / and welked is my face
But sires / to yow / it is no curteisye
To speken / to an old man vileynye   740
But he trespase in word / or ellis in dede
In holy writ / ye may your self wel rede
Agayns an old man / hoor up on his heed
Ye shal arise / wherfore I yeve yow reed
Ne dooth un to an old man / noon harm now   745
Namoore than þt ye wolde / men dide to yow
In age / / if þt ye so longe abyde
And god be with yow / wher ye go or ryde
I moot go thider / as I have to go
Nay olde cherl / by god thow shalt nat so   750
Seyde / this oother hasardour anon
Thow partest nat so lightly / by Seint John
Thow speeke right now / of thilke traytour deeth
That in this contree / alle oure freendes sleeth
Have here my trouthe / as thow art his espye   755
Tel wher he is / or thow shalt it abye

By god / and by the holy sacrament
ffor soothly / thow art oon of his assent
To sleen us yonge folk / thow false theef
Now sires quod he / if þt yow be so leef　　　　760
To fynde deeth / turn up this croked wey
ffor in that grove / I lafte hym by my fey
Under a tree / and ther he wol abyde
Nat for youre boost / he wol hym no thyng hyde
Se ye that ook / right ther ye shal hym fynde　　765
God save yow / that boghte agayn man kynde
And yow amende / thus seyde this olde man
And everich of thise riotours ran
Til he cam to that tree / and ther they founde
Of floryns fyne of gold / ycoyned rounde　　　770
Wel ny an VIII busshels / as hem thoughts
No lenger thanne / after deeth they soughte
But ech of hem / so glad was of the sighte
ffor þt the floryns / been so faire and brighte
That doun they sette hem / by this precious hoord　775
The worste of hem / he spak the firste word
Bretheren quod he / taak kepe / what þt I seye
My wit is greet / thogh þt I bourde and pleye
This tresor hath ffortune / un to us yeven
In myrthe and iolitee / oure lyf to lyven　　　780
And lightly as it cometh / so wol we spende
By goddes precious dignytee / who wende
To day / that we sholde han / so fair a grace
But myghte this gold / be caried fro this place
Hoom to myn hous / or ellis un to youres　　　785
ffor wel ye woot/ that al this gold is oures
Thanne were we / in heigh felicitee
But trewely / by daye it may nat be
Men wolde seyn / þt we were theves stronge
And for oure owene tresor / doon us honge　　　790
This tresor / moste ycaried be by nyghte
As wisly / and as sleyly / as it myghte
Therfore I rede / that cut amonges us alle
Be drawe / and lat se / wher the cut wol falle
And he þt hath the cut / with herte blithe　　　795
Shal renne to towne / and that ful swithe

And brynge us / bred / and wyn / ful prively
And two of us / shal kepen subtilly
This tresor wel / and if he wol nat tarye
Whan it is nyght / we wol this tresor carye   800
By oon assent / wher as us thynketh best
That oon of hem / the cut broghte in his fest
And bad hem drawe / and looke wher it wol falle
And it fel / on the yongeste of hem alle
And forth toward the town / he wente anon   805
And also soone / as þt he was agon
That oon of hem / spak thus un to that oother
Thow knowest wel / thow art my sworn brother
Thy profit / wol I telle thee anon
Thow woost wel / þt oure felawe is agon   810
And heere is gold / and that ful greet plentee
That shal departed been / among us thre
But nathelees / if I kan shape it so
That it departed were / among us two
Hadde I nat doon / a freendes torn to thee   815
That oother answerde / I noot how that may be
He woot þt the gold / is with us tweye
What shal we doon / what shal we to hym seye
Shal it be conseil / seyde the firste shrewe
And I shal telle / in a wordes fewe   820
What we shul doon / and brynge it wel aboute
I graunte quod that oother / out of doute
That by my trouthe / I wol thee nat biwreye
Now quod the firste / thow woost wel we be tweye
And two of us / shul strenger be than oon   825
Looke whan þt he is set / that right anon
Arys / as though thow woldest / with hym pleye
And I shal ryve hym / thurgh the sydes tweye
Whil that thow strogelest with hym / as in game
And with thy daggere / looke thow do the same   830
And thanne shal / al this gold departed be
My deere freend / bitwixe thee and me
Thanne may we bothe / oure lustes al fulfille
And pleye et dees / right at oure owene wille
And thus acorded been / thise sherewes tweye   835
To sleen the thridde / as ye han herd me seye

This yongeste / which that wente to the toun
fful ofte in herte / he rolleth up and doun
The beautee of thise floryns / newe and brighte
O lord quod he / if so were þt I myghte   840
Have al this tresor / to my self allone
Ther is no man / þt lyveth under the trone
Of god / that sholde lyve / so myrie as I
And at the laste / the feend oure enemy
Putte in his thoght / þt he sholde poyson beye   845
With which he myghte sleen / his felawes tweye
ffor why / the feend foond hym / in swich lyvynge
That he hadde leve / hym to sorwe brynge
ffor this was outrely / his ful entente
To sleen hem bothe / and nevere to repente   850
And forth he goth / no lenger wolde he tarye
In to the toun / un to apothecarye
And preyed hym / þt he hym wolde selle
Som poyson / that he myghte his rattes quelle
And eek ther was / a polcat / in his hawe   855
That as he seyde / his capons hadde yslawe
And fayn he wolde / wreke hym if he myghte
On vermyn / that destroyed hym by nyghte
The pothecarie answerde / and thow shalt have
A thyng / that also god / my soule save   860
In all this world / ther is no creature
That ete / or dronke / hath of this confiture
Nat but the montaunce / of a corn of whete
That he ne shal his lyf / anoon for lete
Ye sterve he shal / and that in lasse while   865
Than thow wolt goon a paas / nat but a myle
The poyson / is so strong / and violent
This cursed man / hath in his hand yhent
This poyson in a box / and sith he ran
In to the nexte strete / un to a man   870
And borwed hym / large botels thre
And in the two / his poison poured he
The thridde / he kepte clene for his drynke
ffor al the nyght / he shoop hym for to swynke
In cariyng / of the gold / out of that place   875
And whan this riotour / with sory grace

Hadde filled with wyn / hise grete botels thre
To hise felawes / agayn repaireth he
What nedeth it / to sarmone of it moore
ffor right as they / hadde cast his deeth bifore   880
Right so / they han hym slayn / and that anon
And whan this was doon / thus spak that oon
Now lat us sitte and drynke / and make us merye
And afterward / we wol his body berye
And with that word / it happed hym parcas   885
To take the botel / ther the poyson was
And drank / and yaf his felawe drynke also
ffor which anon / they storven bothe two
But certes I suppose / that Avycen
Wroot nevere in no canon / ne in no fen   890
Mo wonder signes / of empoysonyng
Then hadde thise wrecches two / er hir endyng
Thus ended been / thise homicides two
And eek / the false empoysoner also
O . cursed synne / of alle cursednesse   895
O . traytours homicide / o wikkednesse
O . glotonye / luxure / and hasardrye
Thou blasphemour of Crist / with vileynye
And othes grete / of usage / and of pryde
Allas mankynde / how may it bityde   900
That to thy creatour / which þt thee wroghte
And with his precious herte blood / the boghte
Thow art so fals / and so unkynde allas
Now goode men / god foryeve yow youre trespas
And ware yow / fro the synne of avarice   905
Myn holy pardoun / may yow alle warisse
So that ye offre nobles / or starlynges
Or ellis silver broches / spones / rynges
Boweth your heed / under this holy bulle
Cometh up ye wyves / offreth of youre wolle   910
Youre name I entre / here in my rolle anon
In to the blisse of hevene / shul ye gon
I yow assoille / by myn heigh power
Ye þt wol offre / as clene and eek as cler
As ye were born / and lo sires thus I preche   915
And Jhesu Crist / that is oure soules leche

So graunte yow / his pardoun to receyve
ffor that is best / I wol yow nat deceyve
But sires / o word / forgat I in my tale
I have relikes / and pardon in my male   920
As faire / as any man in Engelond
Whiche were me yeven / by the popes hond
If any of yow / wol of devocioun
Offren / and han my absolucioun
Com forth anon / and kneleth here adoun   925
And mekely / receyveth my pardoun
Or ellis / taketh pardoun as ye wende
Al newe and fressh / at every myles ende
So þt ye offren alwey / newe and newe
Nobles / or pens / whiche þt been goode and trewe   930
It is an honour / to everich that is heer
That ye mowe have / a suffisant pardoner
Tassoille yow / in contree as ye ryde
ffor aventures / whiche þt may bityde
Peraventure / ther may falle oon or two   935
Doun of his hors / and breke his nekke atwo
Looke which a seuretee is it to yow alle
That I am / in youre felaweship yfalle
That may assoille yow / bothe moore and lasse
Whan þt the soule / shal fro the body passe   940
I rede / that oure hoost / shal bigynne
ffor he is moost / envoluped in synne
Com forth sire hoost / and offre first anon
And thow shalt kisse / the relikes everychon
Ye for a grote / unbokele anon thy purs   945
Nay nay quod he / thanne have I Cristes curs
Lat be quod he / it shal nat be so thee ich
Thow woldest / make me kysse thyn olde breech
And swere it were / a relyk of a seint
Thogh it were / with thy fondement depeynt   950
But by the croys / which þt Seint Eleyne foond
I wold I hadde / thy coylons in myn hond
In stide of relikes / or of saintuarie
Lat cutte hem of / I wol thee hem carie
They shul be shryned / in an hogges toord   955
This pardoner / answerde nat a word

So wrooth he was / no word ne wolde he seye
Now quod oure hoost / I wol no lenger pleye
With thee / ne with noon oother angry man
But right anon / the worthy knyght bigan   960
Whan þt he saugh / þt al the peple lough
Namoore of this / for it is right ynough
Sire pardoner be glad / and murye of cheere
And sire hoost / that been to me so deere
I pray yow / þt ye kisse the pardoner   965
And pardoner / I pray thee / drawe thee neer
And as we diden / lat us lawe and pleye
Anon they kiste / and ryden forþ hir weye   968

    In the foregoing transcript of the Hengwrt MS. I have expanded the contractions except for þt. I suggest that the difference between the scribe's use of þt and *that* is a matter of stress. I have, too, written *v* for *u* where the modern pronunciation employs the *v*-phoneme.